P·A·P·E·R

FOR ALL SEASONS

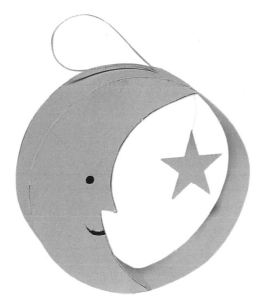

P·A·P·E·R
FOR ALL SEASONS

Projects and Presents to Make Through the Year

Sandra Lounsbury Foose

Photography by Holly McDade

WATSON-GUPTILL
PUBLICATIONS
New York

TO DEAN,
MY LOVE FOR ALL *SEASONS*.

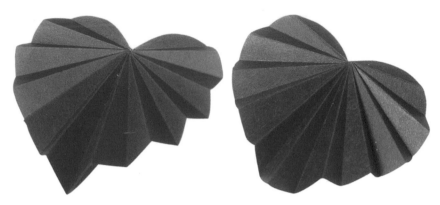

Senior Acquisitions Editor: Joy Aquilino
Project Editor: Michelle Bredeson
Designer: Areta Buk / Thumb Print
Production Manager: Ellen Greene

Published in 2003 by Watson-Guptill Publications,
a division of VNU Business Media, Inc.,
770 Broadway, New York, NY 10003
www.watsonguptill.com

Library of Congress Cataloging-in-Publication Data

Foose, Sandra Lounsbury.
      Paper for all seasons : projects and presents to make through the year
/ Sandra Lounsbury Foose.
            p. cm.
      ISBN 0-8230-3892-0
      1. Paper work. I. Title.
      TT870.F637 2003
      745.54—dc21

                                                2003006940

Manufactured in Malaysia

1 2 3 4 5 6 7 8 9 / 09 08 07 06 05 04 03

When using cutting tools and other suggested products, readers are strongly cautioned to follow
manufacturers' directions, to heed warnings, and to seek prompt medical attention for an injury.
In addition, readers are advised to keep all potentially harmful supplies away from children.

ACKNOWLEDGMENTS

If Winter comes,
Can Spring be far behind?
Percy Bysshe Shelley

As far back as I can remember, I have always loved and celebrated the changing seasons, but it took me a long time to make friends with winter. While growing up in a family of New England gardeners, there were always opportunities for me to witness the magic occurring between seedtime and harvest. Every year on the first day of winter, the darkest, shortest day of the year, I remember my dad announcing, "Spring is coming!" with a confident voice that was almost a shout.

This past winter, as I was completing the final projects for this book, I sat with my dad who, at the age of ninety-three, was living the final days of his life.

From our parents, our first teachers, we learn many things, even when they and we don't realize that the lessons are being imparted. Sometimes the heart and the hands teach us more than spoken words do. From my father's optimistic expectations and my own love of growing things, I have come to understand and appreciate the winter I once so dreaded, as a season of hope, a time for quiet contemplation and creative endeavors. Every year, long before the official date of March 21, I imagine the miracles of creativity stirring beneath the snow and within the barren trees, and I know that spring is coming. Thanks Daddy.

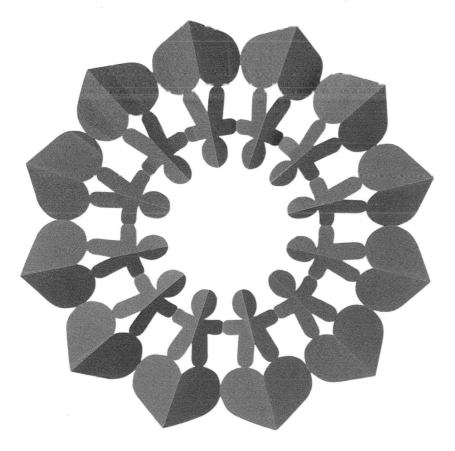

CONTENTS

PREFACE

All beautiful the march of days,
As seasons come and go;
The hand that shaped the rose hath wrought
The crystal of the snow...

Frances Whitmarsh Wile

In the soft sounds and visual poetry of this lovely old hymn, the writer so perfectly expresses her appreciation for the wonder and beauty of every passing day. Beginning in early childhood, we too discover the delights of staying in tune with the seasons as they pass before our eyes in a kaleidoscopic parade. And there are always those unexpected gifts, symbols of the seasons, that appear along the way: purple violets in spring-green grass, seashells washed up on a sandy shore, orange-dotted fields of pick-your-own pumpkins, snowflakes caught on fuzzy mittens, birdsong at daybreak, starlight overhead. Day by day, month by month, as we celebrate the seasons, our celebrations become our traditions, embellishing our memories, and inspiring our future plans.

At home and at school, generations of children have looked to the colors and symbols of the seasons for creative inspiration, taken scissors in hand, and cut paper snowflakes for the windows, paper stars for the ceiling, and paper pumpkins for the walls. Bookstores and libraries are well-stocked with books full of such cut-fold-and-paste projects for children, but there are still places on the shelves for books about paper art for grown-ups. For this very reason, I have written *Paper for All Seasons*, a collection of innovative, yet easy-to-make paper projects with full-size patterns and step-by-step instructions for every design. So, now you too can cut, fold, and paste to your heart's content, creating simple gifts, seasonal decorations, and whimsical greeting cards all through the year.

Creating with paper can be done in a very small space with minimal mess. Your studio can be as close as the kitchen table, and your portfolio can be as simple as a shoebox. How satisfying it is to create with paper: to start or stop on a whim, sweep up a few scraps, tuck away a work in progress, and then return to find it exactly as you left it, ready to complete, instead of encountering dirty paintbrushes or dried out clay. The cost of most paper is negligible, so if you make a mistake, and learn what *cannot* be done with paper, it won't be a big deal to trash the disaster and begin anew. Whether you are seeking the solace of a few creative moments or enhancing your repertoire of imaginative group activities, *Paper for All Seasons* offers you lots of ideas that are affordable and fun, as well as quick and easy to do.

Whenever the season, whatever the reason, may you discover places of inspiration and delight every time you visit the pages of this book. Celebrate the seasons!

CHAPTER ONE

GETTING STARTED

✂

The pleasures of paper are infinite! Paper looks good, it feels good, it even sounds good. It can be as soft as cotton or as crisp as a slice of wood veneer. Paper invites us to cut, fold, twist, curl, crimp, and crumple it. Paper inspires us to play, and the play is magical. Even a tiny paper scrap, a trash-bound "nothing," can be transformed into a delightful "something" when you really love paper. This chapter, an introduction or perhaps a review for you, describes a few members of the enormous paper family, as well as terms, tools, tricks, and techniques for paper pleasure and paper play.

A PAPER PRIMER

Look for paper treasures everywhere! Start with paper stores and card shops, and move on to art and craft centers and mail order catalogs. Then check out discount chains, office suppliers, and party stores. When you travel, especially internationally, look for lovely papers to bring home and add to your collection. Set up your own little paper pantry so you will always have a delectable assortment of ingredients close at hand. Here are some of the many types of paper you will encounter in this book and in your own search.

ART PAPER
These high-quality, heavy-weight papers are made by Canson, Crescent, Canford, Strathmore, Fabriano, and other manufacturers. Richly hued, subtly textured art papers inspire the heart, eye, and hand. Unlike construction paper, which fades easily and splits when scored and folded, art paper holds its color and has good strength and memory.

BOND PAPER
Available in white and a rainbow of wonderful colors, this ordinary, inexpensive, stationery-weight paper usually measures 8 ½ by 11 inches (21.6 by 27.9 cm). Copy shops often carry matching envelopes.

CORRUGATED PAPER
You can sometimes rescue this textured paper from the recycling bin. If the corrugated texture is crushed, repair it by running a thin dowel or a bamboo skewer inside the tunnels to lift up the dents.

DUPLEX PAPER
Also called duet paper, duplex paper is a light- to medium-weight multipurpose paper with a different color, sometimes just white, on each side of a single sheet.

FOIL PAPER AND FOIL BOARD
Smooth and shiny or embossed with texture, metallic foil paper looks wonderful lining envelopes, and that's a great place to salvage it too!

GARDEN PAPER
This soft handmade paper is embedded with real flowers, leaves, and seeds, so no two pieces are ever exactly alike.

GLASSINE
Shiny, transparent, and similar to kitchen wax paper, colorless glassine is used to make envelopes for displaying and protecting paper collectibles such as stamps. Glassine paper is also available in colors, but vellum (described below) is a good substitute if you can't find it.

GLOW-IN-THE-DARK PAPER

Luminescent paper is a pricey splurge, but it sure is fun to use! It cuts and folds like origami paper (described below) and when exposed to light, it glows brightly for at least thirty minutes afterward.

JAPANESE PAPERS

Of the many Japanese papers available, only origami and chiyogami papers were used in this book. Traditional lightweight origami paper is easy to find in packages of brightly colored squares but it is also available in metallic foil, double-sided, iridescent, luminescent, opalescent, and Japanese folk-art print assortments. Brilliantly colored chiyogami paper is silk-screened with exquisite repeating patterns. It is medium-weight, fade-resistant, and strong, yet soft to the touch.

KRAFT PAPER

Humble but handsome and easy to salvage, kraft paper is most often used for bagging groceries and wrapping parcels because of its strength and low cost. Now and then you may encounter kraft paper enhanced with a printed design or brushed with a metallic wash, and the look is surprisingly elegant.

PAPER DOILIES

Frosty white circles, squares, rectangles, ovals, and hearts of paper lace can be found in card shops, supermarkets, and places that sell party supplies.

QUILLING STRIPS

Available in a wonderful assortment of colors, quilling strips are very narrow, precision-cut pieces of paper. In addition to quilling (a papercraft not included in this book), the strips are perfect for weaving and for adding decorative touches to projects such as party hats.

SCRAPBOOKING PAPERS

These beautifully colored, patterned, and embossed papers are sold singly, in booklets, or in packs, and they are absolutely irresistible!

VELLUM

A medium-weight, high-quality, transparent paper, vellum is stronger than ordinary tracing paper. It makes interesting transparent envelopes that can actually be sent through the mail. Vellum is available in colors and with printed or embossed patterns on it.

VELOUR PAPER AND VELOUR BOARD

Flocked velour paper has a soft, fuzzy, suede-like finish, which adds a pleasing tactile quality to your work.

WALLPAPER

Uncoated sheets of upscale wallpaper cut from an old sample book were used to make several of the projects in this book. Wallpaper samples also make wonderful note cards, place mats, shelf liners, book covers, photo mats, and gift wraps.

COLLECTING SCRAPS

Without spending a single penny you can create a fabulous paper palette from scraps, leftovers, and throwaways.

Gift-giving occasions yield wrappings and boxes, ribbons and strings, as well as the colorful paper of greeting cards, envelopes, and their linings. Packaging materials worth salvaging could be lurking just inside the shopping bags and other merchandise you regularly carry home. Even the mailbox holds potential treasures in the form of advertisements, invitations, annual reports, garden catalogs, promotional mailings, and such. Check for unusual colors, patterns, and textures on folders, bags, stationery, calendars, playing cards, newspapers, maps, the covers of old notebooks, paint chip cards, damaged sheets of music, and even the corrugated inserts of lightbulb cartons and cosmetic boxes.

Search your community for other freebies. Many of the patterned papers you will see in this book were found in discontinued wallpaper sample books about to be discarded by an interior design shop in my small town. Local printers, paper superstores, and paper wholesalers might have outdated or duplicate paper sample books that could be yours for the asking. After carefully removing the samples from the books (watch those staples), you will often find that the swatches are large enough to make complete projects.

THE WORKBOX

Collect all of these pieces of basic equipment and stash them together in a toolbox, sturdy basket, tote bag, or plastic storage container. If there are little children in your home, be sure to keep your workbox out of their reach. Every time you make a project you will need to use at least one item from your workbox, so most of the tools in the workbox won't appear again on the materials list provided for each project.

ACETATE
Strong, transparent acetate is used to make sturdy, long-lasting patterns. Although it can be purchased, it is easy to scavenge from packaging components such as gift box lids.

CLIP CLOTHESPINS
Hold glued pieces of paper together with clothespins while they dry. Use clothespins as giant paper clips to keep your patterns, papers, and notes organized.

COMPASS
An ordinary pencil-holding compass is adequate for drawing circles, but a multiuse clip compass is even better because it will hold a marker or a craft knife. For the greatest cutting accuracy, however, an adjustable-arm circle cutter is the best.

COTTON SWABS
Dampened just a little bit, a cotton swab is perfect for removing glue spots. Cotton swabs also work as extensions of your fingertips for flattening glue tabs inside of three-dimensional forms.

CRAFT KNIFE AND REPLACEMENT BLADES
Scissors can be used for some of the projects, but many designs require the use of a craft knife with a No. 11 blade. Select a knife with a soft, rubberized (preferably contoured) barrel for comfort and control, and an anti-roll device and a cap for safety. The knife should also have a safe and easy blade-release mechanism. In order to protect your most precious tools—your own two hands—avoid all other cutting devices.

CUTTING MAT
Heavy cardboard can be used as a temporary cutting mat, but it wears out quickly and dulls the blade of your craft knife. Some self-healing cutting mats are really made for rotary cutters, and they forget how to heal when a craft blade mars the surface. The best cutting base has a translucent, semi-hard, rubber-like surface that accepts the blade and then miraculously heals itself. Choose a non-slip mat that is conveniently marked with a grid pattern. The one I have heals so completely that I use it as both a drawing board and a cutting surface.

ERASER
With gentle pressure, a nonabrasive white vinyl eraser removes pencil lines cleanly, without smudging. For precise work the most convenient form is an eraser that resembles a mechanical pencil.

FELT TIP PENS

An inexpensive, basic set of fine-line markers is adequate. Test markers on your project paper to check for feathering of color.

GLUE

Elmer's All-Purpose Glue Stick dries clear and makes a strong bond. It also dries quickly but not instantly, so if you work fast you can make small adjustments. Always try a test patch of glue on your good paper and allow it to dry.

MONOFILAMENT

This soft, invisible, nylon sewing thread is used to make hanging loops for some of the ornament projects.

NEEDLES AND PINS

Needles and pins are used to pierce holes in patterns so construction details can be inconspicuously transferred onto your good paper with tiny pencil dots. Pins and needles are also used to make holes or pierced design details directly on a project, so you should have a variety of sizes, some quite thin and some chunky. "T" pins are a good choice, because the bar at the top serves as a kind of a handle, making the pin easy to hold.

PAPER CLIPS

These little helpers can hold tracing paper in place on the book page while you are drawing a pattern. Paper clips can also anchor your pattern on your good paper and hold glued layers of paper together to dry. Use them with care to avoid scratching your work, and remove them promptly to avoid any rust marks.

PAPER PUNCHES

Metal plier-type paper punches are available in 1/16-inch (0.2-cm), 1/8-inch (0.3-cm), 3/16-inch (0.5-cm), and 1/4-inch (0.6-cm) circle diameters. All four sizes are used in this book, but if you have trouble finding the 3/16-inch (0.5-cm) diameter, the 1/4-inch (0.6-cm) size can usually be substituted. Decorative punches produce a variety of cut confetti shapes, such as hearts, stars, and butterflies.

The following items are not essential, but they would be useful additions to your workbox.

Bone Folder
Blunt at one end and somewhat pointed at the other, a bone folder dragged across your work helps you to make better creases when folding paper.

Drawing Board
A drawing board with a T-square and triangles is not a must, but such supplies do ensure accuracy and efficiency. If you consider such a purchase, a plastic studio drawing board with a paper clamp and a removable transparent sliding straightedge that acts as a T-square is affordable and more than adequate. To complete the set, use inexpensive 45- and 60-degree plastic triangles on the board. Neither the plastic board nor the plastic triangles should be used with a craft knife.

Erasable Transfer Paper
Used like carbon paper to transfer pattern details, transfer paper is waxless, greaseless, and smudge-proof. Graphite and white transfer paper are available in reusable sheets and rolls. It's best to have one sheet of each color. If you do not purchase transfer paper, refer to "Transferring Details" on page 17 for other methods.

Paper Crimper
When smooth paper is inserted and rotated between the rollers of this clever hand tool the paper obtains a corrugated texture.

PENCILS AND SHARPENER

Use a No. 2 wooden school pencil with a soft graphite lead to trace patterns and transfer patterns onto paper, and a white coloring pencil to transfer patterns onto dark paper. A quality handheld sharpener with a twist-off barrel to empty shavings will help to keep your work area neat.

RULER

I use a 6-inch (15.2 cm) or 12-inch (30.5 cm) ruler for most projects. A safety ruler serves double-duty as a measuring device as well as a straightedge when cutting with a craft knife. Safety rulers have nonskid backings and are designed so there is a barrier between your fingers and the knife.

SCISSORS

When selecting scissors, consider comfort as well as size. Try them before you buy them. For general use I favor lightweight, all-purpose, 7-inch (17.8-cm) scissors, with molded plastic handles. For delicate and precise work I use 5-inch (12.7-cm) pointed-tip embroidery scissors. Paper edgers are used for cutting decorative borders. Dozens of designs are available, but only the scalloped and the zigzag edgers were used in this book.

STRAIGHTEDGE

An 18-inch (45.7-cm) or a 24-inch (61.0-cm) metal straightedge is required to safely cut paper with a craft knife. It must protect your fingers, so look for one with a nonskid backing and a barrier or lip on one of its edges.

STYLUS

This tool is used for creating embossed lines as well as folding lines. Sometimes a dull table knife can be substituted.

TAPE

Transparent tape is occasionally used to hold paper pieces together and to reinforce delicate scoring lines. Removable tape is used when making patterns and attaching patterns to your good paper.

TOOTHPICKS

When adding bits of glue in tight places, toothpicks are helpful little tools.

TRACING PAPER

As an alternative to photocopying, use this lightweight, transparent paper to trace the patterns directly from the book.

TWEEZERS

Use tweezers to move tiny pieces of paper into position and to hold hard-to-reach layers of paper together while drying.

TRICKS AND TECHNIQUES

"If all else fails, read the directions." I don't know who first offered that advice, but I know many who take it to heart! The best lessons do sometimes come from our worst mistakes, but taking the time to review basic information at the beginning of an activity is a better way to learn, so please read on.

MAKING PATTERNS

Some projects are best made with photocopied patterns, but most can be traced directly from the book. Hold the tracing paper on the page with paper clips or removable tape and trace accurately. Note that on the patterns continuous solid lines are always cutting lines, dotted lines show placement of a detail or another piece, and broken lines indicate folding lines.

To strengthen patterns or make very tiny ones easier to handle, glue the pieces to acetate before cutting them out. When using a craft knife, it is not always necessary to cut through the acetate; just score it on the pattern line and then complete the job by breaking the acetate on the scored line.

TRANSFERRING DETAILS

Pattern details can be transferred onto your project paper in several ways. One method involves using a needle or a pin to pierce the pattern details, such as folding lines, before the pattern is placed on your project paper. The details can then be transferred directly onto the project paper by placing pencil dots inside the pattern holes.

Using erasable transfer paper is another option. Transfer paper is very responsive to pressure, so draw gently over the pattern lines, but always test the product on a scrap of your good paper before you use it.

One more method is to trace and cut out the pattern, flip it over, and, with a pencil, redraw the details on the reverse side of the pattern, right on top of the original detail lines. Then flip the pattern over again so the right side of it faces you. Place the pattern on the paper of your choice. Draw around the pattern and transfer the details to your good paper by drawing on top of the pattern detail lines again.

DETERMINING PAPER GRAIN

Most papers have a grain, which is a built-in directional preference based on the arrangement of the paper fibers. This structural quality makes it easier to fold or tear paper in one direction than in the other, say top to bottom, rather than side to side. Creasing a paper "with the grain" makes the cleanest folding line. Folds made across or "against the grain" sometimes appear uneven and ragged. When folds must be made in both directions, scoring the paper before folding it will help to ensure a good appearance. To test a paper's grain, bring two of its parallel edges together, bending the paper at the middle without folding it. Then release the bend, rotate the paper a quarter turn, and bring the remaining two parallel edges together. The paper will be easier to bend in one direction than the other. The grain runs parallel to the edges that are easiest to bring together. A fold made parallel to those edges is made "with the grain."

USING TAPE

Use removable tape or paper clips to hold patterns on your project paper, but first make a test patch of tape on your good paper to see if it mars the surface or leaves a sticky residue. Removable tape *is* easy to remove, but if it is left in place for even a short time it will leave a sticky residue that is *not* easy to remove.

ERASING DRAWINGS

Rough erasing will mar or tear the surface of some papers and remove the color or make shiny spots on others. Make slow gentle strokes in one direction, instead of scrubbing the area in a fury. Use a light touch when drawing so you won't need to remove heavy lines.

CUTTING PAPER

Practice cutting scraps with a craft knife, and find the way to hold it that gives you the greatest control and comfort.

To cut or score straight lines, always use a nonslip safety ruler or straightedge as a barrier between your fingers and the craft knife. When cutting or scoring curved lines, keep moving the paper, instead of the knife, and place your fingers away from the path of the blade. If working on a small piece of paper brings your hand too close to the knife, securely tape the small piece of paper onto a bigger piece. Always keep your eyes and your full attention on the blade.

When cutting multiple duplicate shapes together, stack the papers and use tape or clips to hold each layer of paper securely to the next. If the layers are not bound together, they will shift as pressure is applied on the knife, and distorted shapes will result. When cutting through multiple layers of paper, it is safer to make several successive cuts with gentle pressure rather than trying to cut through all the layers with one heavy-handed pass of the knife. It is hazardous to use a dull blade or one with even a tiny piece of the tip broken off. These conditions diminish your control of the knife and they might ruin the paper, tearing it instead of cutting it. Carefully wrap a used blade in tape before disposing of it responsibly.

For the greatest accuracy when cutting curves with scissors, keep the scissors stationary, and move the paper into the cutting blades, instead of keeping the paper stationary and moving the scissors around it.

SCORING AND FOLDING

Medium-weight and heavy paper must be scored in order to fold neatly. Move the craft knife along an accurately drawn folding line (broken line on pattern), making a very shallow groove in the paper without cutting through it. Within the groove, the knife breaks only the very top fibers of the paper, enabling you to fold it precisely. When scoring curved lines, move the paper instead of the knife as you follow the line. It is easiest to score small pieces before they are cut out.

Some projects require scoring on the front of the piece; others need scoring on the reverse side. The instructions will tell you

Treat your paper collection with care. Store the sheets flat. You can make a hinged storage portfolio for large papers by using wide tape to join two same-size pieces of cardboard together along one edge. Sort smaller pieces of paper by color in folders, bags, or envelopes, but before you squirrel them away, remove all traces of tape so the adhesive residue will not mar the texture or discolor the paper surface.

Rolling paper for storage is not a good idea, but if you absolutely must do it, roll the pieces very loosely and don't put rubber bands, tape, or paper clips on them. Instead, wrap a strip of scrap paper around the roll and use a piece of tape to attach the strip to itself. If paper is difficult to flatten after being rolled, gently roll it in the opposite direction.

Keep paper out of the sun and away from moisture and make sure your hands are very clean and dry before you touch it. Dust, finger-prints, and graphite smudges are difficult to remove; color fading is irreversible.

Although it is easier said than done, keep your work area neat and clean. Only set up the items you need for the project at hand and keep your tools clean too. Replace the cap on the glue. Store your tapes in plastic bags to keep the edges clean. Wash your hands after using pencils and glue. And don't use your drawing board for a snack tray!

when and where to score. Paper is usually bent away from a scored line. When you see the term "mountain fold," mark and score the folding line on the right side of the paper and then bend the paper away from you to create the peak of an imaginary mountain. When you see the term "valley fold," mark and score the folding line on the reverse side of the paper, then flip the paper over to the right side and bend it toward you to make a little valley. To create an accordion-folded piece of paper, make alternating parallel mountain and valley folds on it. To protect your paper, use a cover sheet of tracing paper over your work when creasing or flattening it.

Be careful when scoring and folding wallpaper, because it may crack. Mend or reinforce a weak area by placing a piece of transparent tape on the reverse side of the trouble spot.

USING GLUE

Sometimes glue can change the color of a paper or bubble its surface, so always make a test patch on your good paper, and allow it to dry thoroughly before you proceed. Spread a thin layer of glue quickly and uniformly, using a toothpick, craft stick, or folded index card as a tool, depending on the size of your work. After joining glued surfaces, place a clean sheet of tracing paper (a cover sheet) over the work to protect it, and then rub the area to smooth it and distribute the glue. Do the smoothing with your fingertips, or roll a glue-stick tube on it, or pull your straightedge or bone folder over the work. Then remove the cover sheet and use paper clips or clothespins to hold the glued areas together until dry. Alternatively, sandwich the piece between two layers of tracing paper and place it under a stack of heavy books. Elmer's All-Purpose Glue Stick will dry clear, but if it leaves shiny spots on your work, use a damp, not wet, cotton swab to carefully wipe away the dried glue. Keep the opposite cotton end dry so it can be used to smooth the dampened area and absorb excess moisture. First try the dampened swab on a scrap piece to see if moisture mars the paper surface or causes the color to bleed. Sometimes it's just better to leave the glue spot.

CHAPTER TWO

SPRING CELEBRATIONS

♥

Open up the windows and welcome the arrival of spring, when each day brings more light, more warmth, and more color into our lives. Much like the season itself, this chapter is filled with lots of surprises and sentimental celebrations of the heart. Spring cleaning can wait for another day! It's time to bring out the paper, find your scissors, and make some hearts and flowers, bunnies and butterflies. Just turn the page and you will find an endearing collection of valentines, baby things, Easter projects, note cards, garlands, and party favors.

HUGS AND KISSES CARD

Practice sending the most perfect hugs and kisses using the traditional handwriting exercises of yesteryear. This valentine, somewhat reminiscent of a third grade love note, couldn't be simpler to make. Just photocopy the pattern and draw colored ruling lines directly on the photocopy so it will look like notebook paper. Then write "hugs and kisses" inside the folded photocopy and don't forget to add a gold star at the top!

♥

1   The photocopy of the pattern will also be the card. At the copy shop ask for "card stock" in place of bond paper. Do not cut out the photocopied valentine.

2   Using the marks around the edge of the heart as guides, draw horizontal blue lines directly on the photocopy with the blue felt tip pen and ruler. The broken lines on the border indicate the position of the broken lines on the valentine. Using the double marks at the top and the bottom of the heart's left edge as guides, draw double red vertical lines on the photocopy.

3   Score and fold the paper along the broken line at the top of the heart. Clip or tape the edges of the folded paper together and cut out the heart on the outline. Place a gold star at the top. Trace the "hugs and kisses" message and transfer it to the inside of the card, if you wish.

MATERIALS

For one 4 1/2- by 4 3/16-inch (11.4- by 10.6-cm) card

Photocopy of pattern on page 90

Blue and red fine-line felt tip pens

Gold star sticker, optional

Envelope, 4 1/4 by 5 1/8 inches (10.8 by 13.0 cm), or Envelope C pattern, page 88, and instructions, pages 86 to 87

NOTE: *The liner for the envelope was made from a paper layer peeled off the back of a discarded notebook.*

SUPERSONIC VALENTINE

*S*end a love note to your valentine via airmail! Fold your message into a form that really flies, trailing little hearts in its wake. The glider flies best when the wings are in a perfectly horizontal position. For launching, use your thumb and forefinger to hold the glider on the bottom near the front, as you point the nose up, and throw it gently. Otherwise, use an envelope.

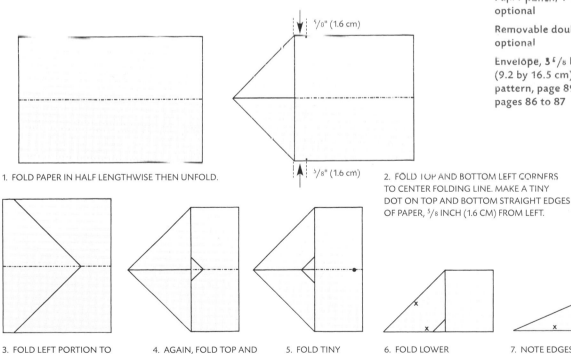

1 There is no pattern for this project. Refer to drawings 1 through 7, below, to make the glider with your practice paper, creasing all the folds sharply. Determine the best place for your written message.

2 Make the glider again with your good paper, completing steps 1 through 5. At this point, punch out or hand cut three 1-inch (2.5-cm) paper hearts and glue them to the monofilament. Referring to drawing 5, glue the monofilament at the dot on the center folding line.

3 Complete the glider referring to drawings 6 and 7. If the glider won't stay folded, tuck a small piece of removable double-sided tape between the paper layers at the center top or add a tiny sticker at the center top to keep the layers together.

MATERIALS

For one 2 1/4- by 6 1/2-inch (5.7- by 16.5-cm) glider

One 6 1/2- by 9 1/2-inch (16.5- by 24.1-cm) piece of bond-weight duplex paper for glider, and one for practice

Scrap paper for hearts

8-inch (20.3-cm) length of monofilament

Paper punch, 1-inch (2.5-cm) heart, optional

Removable double-sided tape, optional

Envelope, 3 5/8 by 6 1/2 inches (9.2 by 16.5 cm), or Envelope D pattern, page 89, and instructions, pages 86 to 87

1. FOLD PAPER IN HALF LENGTHWISE THEN UNFOLD.

5/8" (1.6 cm)

2. FOLD TOP AND BOTTOM LEFT CORNERS TO CENTER FOLDING LINE. MAKE A TINY DOT ON TOP AND BOTTOM STRAIGHT EDGES OF PAPER, 5/8 INCH (1.6 CM) FROM LEFT.

3. FOLD LEFT PORTION TO RIGHT, MAKING FOLDING LINE AT DOT PLACEMENT POINTS ON TOP AND BOTTOM EDGES.

4. AGAIN, FOLD TOP AND BOTTOM CORNERS TO CENTER FOLDING LINE.

5. FOLD TINY TRIANGLE TO LEFT.

6. FOLD LOWER PORTION TO BACK SO CENTER FOLDING LINE IS AT BOTTOM OF GLIDER.

7. NOTE EDGES MARKED "X" IN DRAWING 6. FOLD DOWN EACH WING OF GLIDER SO X EDGES ALIGN. RAISE WINGS TO A HORIZONTAL POSITION BEFORE FLYING.

PLEATED HEART ORNAMENT

A heart-shaped scallop shell, polished and sculpted by the sea and found on a beach on Nantucket, provided the inspiration for this ornament. To make the design an honest to goodness quick and easy project, use good quality origami or bond paper. Otherwise, the pleats will split apart when the paper is accordion-folded. If you use duplex paper, the heart will be especially pretty when it turns and spins around. The ornament looks best when it is made this size or smaller.

♥

1 Photocopy or trace the pattern and cut it out. Pierce the dot with a pin.

2 Attach the pattern to the paper with removable tape or paper clips. Trace around the shape. Transfer the dot with a sharp pencil placed in the pinhole. Mark the pleats around the heart shape with dots. Remove the pattern.

3 Before cutting out the heart, lightly draw the pleat lines on the right side of the paper. Connect the dots from one edge of the heart to the opposite edge of the heart, making one continuous line that passes through the center dot.

4 Cut out the heart shape, but do not cut the top crevice all the way down to the dot at this time. Make mountain folds on all of the pleat lines, making a continuous fold from one edge of the heart, through the center dot and then to the opposite edge of the heart. Each of the two pleats marked with an X folds only to the center dot of the heart, and not to the opposite edge. Be gentle with the work.

5 Flip the heart over to the reverse side and refold the creases, making mountain folds on this side. Carefully cut the top crevice down to the dot. Place the heart right side up on your work surface and fold it again in the following way making sharp creases, and handling the work gently. Start at the center with a mountain fold. Then make a valley fold on one of the X-marked pleats adjacent to the center mountain fold. Continue accordion-folding the rest of the pleats on one side of the heart, and then the other. If the paper weakens at the top crevice, reinforce it with a very tiny spot of glue placed on the reverse side of the heart after you have completed the accordion folding.

6 On the reverse side of the heart the center fold will be a valley fold. Place a dot of glue on the end of a single strand of monofilament. Tuck it into the center valley fold with the help of a toothpick. When the glue is dry, make a small loop at the opposite end of the monofilament to hang the ornament.

MATERIALS

For one 2 1/8- by 2 3/8-inch
(5.4- by 6.0-cm) ornament

Pattern on page 91

3 1/4-inch (8.3-cm) square of paper

10-inch (25.4-cm) length of
monofilament

NESTED HEARTS ORNAMENT

Three little strips of paper and a few drops of glue are all you need to create this ornament for Valentine's Day. With a change of colors it can be a quick and easy decoration to make for weddings, anniversaries, baby showers, birthdays, and even Christmas!

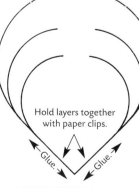

1 Photocopy or trace the patterns for the three heart strips and glue the patterns to acetate if you wish. Cut out the patterns, piercing a few dots along the tip folding line and the glue areas. Also pierce the hanging loop placement dot on the pattern for heart 1.
2 Use paper clips to hold the patterns against the paper strips and use a sharp pencil to transfer the folding lines, glue areas, and hanger dot.
3 Score and crease the tip folding line on each strip. Place the strip for heart 1 on your work surface so that the folding line is in a valley fold position. Spread glue within the shaded center area and place the strip for heart 2 on top of the strip for heart 1. Align the folding lines and the long edges of the strips. Spread glue within the shaded center area on the strip for heart 2 and top it with the strip for heart 3. Again align the folding lines and the long edges of the strips. Place paper clips on the glued areas to flatten the paper layers and allow the glue to dry completely. The front view of the unit should resemble drawing 1, below.
4 Glue the shaded ends of the strips together as in drawing 2. Align the edges carefully and hold the layers together with paper clips until they are completely dry.
5 Glue the monofilament hanging loop in place at the dot on heart 1. Glue the layered ends of the strips together at the center top of the heart.

MATERIALS

For one 2 1/2-inch (6.4-cm) ornament

Patterns on page 91

3/4- by 9-inch (1.9- by 22.9-cm) piece of paper for heart 1

3/4- by 7 1/2-inch (1.9- by 19.1-cm) piece of paper for heart 2

3/4- by 6-inch (1.9- by 15.2-cm) piece of paper for heart 3

10-inch (25.4-cm) length of monofilament

Hold layers together with paper clips.

1. GLUE LAYERS TOGETHER NEAR TIP.

Glue.   Glue.

Hold layers together with paper clips.

2. GLUE ENDS TOGETHER.

LOOPED HEARTS GARLAND

MATERIALS

For one 36-inch (91.4-cm) garland

6 1/2- by 10 1/2-inch (16.9- by 26.6-cm) piece of paper for thirteen hearts

4 3/8- by 6-inch (11.1- by 15.6-cm) piece of paper for twelve links

Candy-colored hearts are linked together to make this quick paper garland. There are no patterns to trace or copy here, but you do need to draw and glue the pieces together accurately, of course. The materials listed are for making a chain of one or two colors. To create a multi-colored chain, use paper scraps of several different colors or prints.

1 There are no patterns for this project. To make the hearts, refer to drawing 1, below, and draw the thirteen heart strips. Lightly mark the glue areas with a pencil line and score the folding lines with a craft knife. Cut the strips apart on the solid horizontal lines.

2 To assemble each heart, refer to drawing 2. Crease the center line as well as the glue tab lines at the end of each strip. Spread a small amount of glue on the shaded glue area at the end of each strip. Curve the strip into a heart shape as shown in drawing 2. Hold the double-layered center section of the heart together with paper clips until the glue dries.

3 To make the links, draw and cut twelve 1/2- by 4 3/8-inch (1.3- by 11.1-cm) strips. Spread a small amount of glue at one end of one link strip. Pass the strip through two hearts and overlap the ends of the strip 1/4 inch (0.6 cm) to form a ring. Hold until dry. Continue until all the hearts are joined.

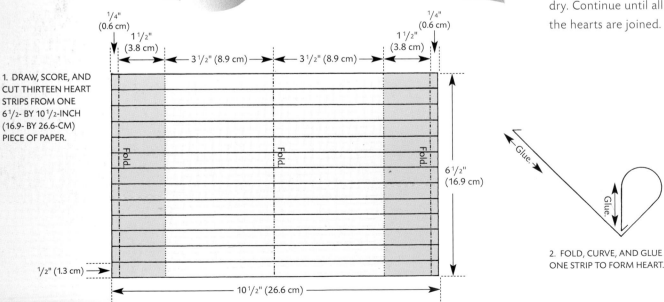

1. DRAW, SCORE, AND CUT THIRTEEN HEART STRIPS FROM ONE 6 1/2- BY 10 1/2-INCH (16.9- BY 26.6-CM) PIECE OF PAPER.

2. FOLD, CURVE, AND GLUE ONE STRIP TO FORM HEART.

CANDY HEART BASKET

"True Love," "Be Mine," "Call Me," "Cutie Pie." Tiny conversation hearts are such a part of Valentine's Day memories! Their soft pastel colors, just as sweet as the candies themselves, are used to make these quick and easy baskets. Fill the baskets with small gifts for your valentine, or use them for party favors at showers, weddings, anniversaries, and other romantic occasions.

♥

1 Photocopy or trace the patterns and cut them out. Pierce the folding lines in a few places with a pin.

2 Place the heart pattern on the heart paper and anchor the layers together with removable tape or paper clips. Trace around the outside edge, drawing two hearts. Cut out both. From one paper strip, cut one bow, one streamer piece, and one knot. Reserve the remaining strip, as is, for the handle. Transfer all of the folding and placement lines with pencil dots. Cut out the pieces. Score and crease the folding lines on the right side of the paper. Mark the center point at 6 1/4 inches (15.9 cm) on both sides of the reserved handle strip. This will be the center top of the handle.

3 Apply glue to the right side of the glue tab along one edge of one heart. Align one end of the handle strip with the tip of the heart. Align one long edge of the handle with the straight edge of the heart. Press the handle against the heart tab until the glue is dry.

4 Apply glue to the right side of the paper on the glue tab along the remaining straight edge of the same heart. Arch the handle over the heart top and then align one free edge of the handle with the remaining straight edge of the heart. Also align the end of the handle at the heart tip, the center bottom of the basket. Press the handle against the heart tab until the glue is dry. Repeat to add the second heart to the other edge of the handle.

5 Curl the ends of the streamer piece, and put it aside. Apply a small amount of glue to the reverse side of each end of the bow strip. Bring the ends to the center and butt them together. Allow the glue to dry. Glue the bow to the center of the streamer piece. Glue the bow unit to the handle. Place the knot piece on top of the bow. Fold the ends of the knot to the underside of the handle, and glue them in place.

MATERIALS

For one 3 5/8- by 5- by 5/8-inch (9.2- by 12.75- by 1.6-cm) basket

Patterns on page 92

3 1/2- by 7-inch (8.9- by 17.8-cm) piece of sturdy paper for heart shapes

Two 5/8- by 12 1/2-inch (1.6- by 31.8-cm) pieces of sturdy paper for handle, bow, knot, and streamer piece

BABY BOOTIES

Looking like tiny espadrilles, these petite booties could embellish a present, carry a gift certificate, hold party mints, or decorate a Christmas tree. Directions for making the scallop edge booties are at the end of the instructions and you should read through them before you cut your paper.

♥

1 Photocopy or trace the patterns and cut them out. On the side piece, use a pin to pierce the center back dot, as well as the placement lines for the long glue tabs and the back strap. On the vamp, pierce the center front dot. On the sole pattern, pierce the center front and center back dots.

2 Using removable tape or paper clips, place the side, vamp, and strap patterns on the bootie paper. Trace around each shape and place a sharp pencil in the pierced holes to transfer the placement lines and center dots. After removing the pattern from the work, lightly draw the long glue tab lines on the ends of the side piece. Also draw a continuous line at the base of the glue tabs on both the vamp and the side pieces to provide a guideline for scoring. Draw two sole pieces on the contrasting paper, transferring the center front and center back dots to the right side and reverse side of each piece.

3 On the right side of the paper, use a craft knife to lightly score a continuous line on the broken lines along the base of the small glue tabs on both the vamp and the side piece. Next, cut the solid lines between the small tabs. Finally, cut along the sides of the small tabs. Continue to cut out all of the bootie pieces.

MATERIALS

For two booties, each 1 ¹/₈ by 1 ¹/₂ by 2 ⁷/₈ inches (2.9 by 3.8 by 7.3 cm)

Patterns on page 95

7-inch (17.8-cm) square of paper for upper portions of booties

3 ¹/₂- by 7-inch (8.9- by 17.8-cm) piece of contrasting paper for bootie soles and insoles

Two 13 ¹/₂-inch (34.3-cm) lengths of ¹/₈-inch (0.3) wide ribbon

4   On the right side of the side piece, spread glue on the two long glue tabs. Overlap the tabs with the vamp piece and hold until dry. On the reverse side of one of the sole pieces, spread a ¼-inch (0.6 cm) margin of glue around the edge. This piece will be the insole. Working from the bottom, hold the insole inside of the bootie so that the glue-edged surface of the insole faces you and the center front and center back dots align with the dots on the vamp and side piece. Fold down the center front and center back glue tabs, overlapping the insole. Use tiny pieces of transparent tape to anchor these two tabs to the insole. Glue the remaining tabs to the insole. Place the bootie flat on the work surface. To flatten the insole against the glue tabs, place one end of a cotton swab inside the bootie and press down all around the insole.

5   Turn the bootie upside down again and spread glue on the reverse side of the insole, right over the glue tabs. Working from the bottom, place the sole on the insole, sandwiching the glue tabs in between the two layers. When the glue has dried, look for areas where the sole extends beyond the bootie and carefully trim away the excess. At the center back of the side piece, apply a narrow band of glue to the inside and outside of the bootie. Place the back strap on the glue bands inside and outside the bootie, leaving a loop at the top edge of the center back. Thread one end of one ribbon piece through the loop. Repeat steps 2 through 5, above, to make the other bootie.

6   To make the scallop-trimmed edges on the booties, first draw the pattern pieces on the reverse side of the paper. Before cutting out the pieces use a craft knife to score, but not cut, the top edges of the vamp and side piece. Then use decorative-edge scissors to cut only those two edges, just beyond the scored lines. The crevice of the scallop cuts should almost touch the scored line. Fold the scallops to the right side of the paper and flatten them there. Cut the remaining edges with the craft knife.

TOY KEYS CARD

This classic rattle has been a favorite baby toy for years and years. Made with pastel papers it also works well as a playful note card. Add words of greeting to each key or express your good wishes in a circle around the ring.

♥

1 Trace or photocopy the patterns and cut them out. On the white paper, draw the key ring and cut it out, using a craft knife on a protected work surface. Cut out the center circle and cut through the ring as indicated with a solid line on the pattern.

2 On each colored paper, trace one different key shape and cut it out. Slip each key onto the ring. Close the ring with a small circle of white paper cut with the paper punch and glued over the opening. Allow the piece to dry. Pull the keys around the ring to cover the patched area.

MATERIALS

For one 3 1/8- by 6-inch (7.9- by 15.2-cm) card

Patterns on page 93

3 1/2-inch (8.9-cm) square of sturdy white paper

Four 2 1/2- by 4-inch (6.4- by 10.2-cm) pieces of different sturdy pastel-colored papers

Paper punch, 1/4-inch (0.6-cm) diameter

Envelope, 4 1/4 by 5 1/8 inches (10.8 by 13.0 cm), or Envelope C pattern, page 88, and instructions, pages 86 to 87

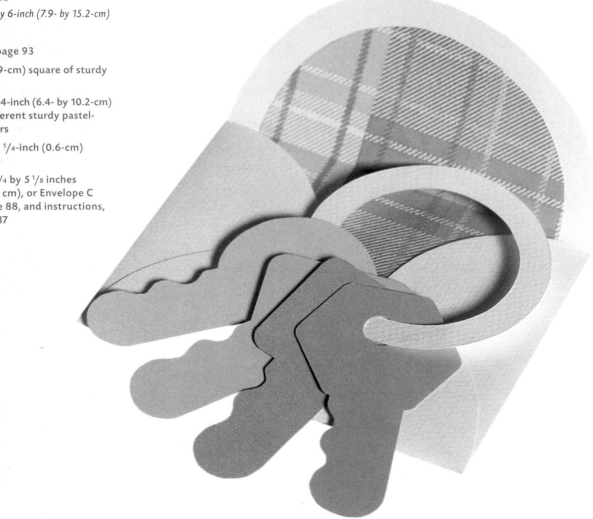

MARSHMALLOW BUNNIES

Two sure signs of spring are the appearance of the first crocus and the return of the marshmallow bunnies! The bunnies look just as cute tucked into an Easter envelope as they do peeking out of a wicker basket or a tiny top hat. Make a paper grass nest for them in a translucent vellum envelope and sprinkle the grass with a few bright punched-out circles to suggest jelly beans. Follow the directions to make your choice of a garland, note card, or place card.

♥

NOTE CARD

1 Photocopy or trace the patterns and cut them out. Cut out the circles for the eyes and the nose with the paper punch or a craft knife.

2 Score and fold the paper in half. Align the "place on fold" edge of the pattern with the folded edge of the card, holding the pattern in place with removable tape or paper clips. Draw around the shape and within the eyes and noses. Remove the pattern.

3 Secure the folded card layers together with tape or clips. Cut out the bunnies. Add color to the eyes and noses with the felt tip pen.

PLACE CARD

To make a bunny place card, trace the single bunny pattern and follow the instructions for the note card.

GARLAND

Fold the garland paper in half crosswise and unfold it. Then fold the short edges to the center folding line and unfold. Accordion-fold the paper on the folding lines you have created. Place the single bunny pattern on the folded paper so the bunny sides align with the folded edges. Trace around the pattern, remove it, and cut out the bunny shape. Add glue and glitter, if you wish. To make a longer garland, join short garlands together, side by side, with tape placed on the reverse side.

MATERIALS

For one 2 5/8- by 5 1/8-inch (6.7- by 13.0-cm) note card; one 1 3/4- by 3-inch (4.4- by 7.6-cm) place card; or one 2 3/4- by 5-inch (7.0- by 12.7-cm) garland

Patterns on page 92

6-inch (15.2-cm) square of sturdy yellow paper for note card

1 3/4- by 6-inch (4.4- by 15.2-cm) piece of sturdy yellow paper for place card

3 1/4- by 5-inch (8.3-by 12.7-cm) piece of sturdy yellow paper for garland

Tan or beige fine line felt tip pen

Paper punch, 1/16-inch (0.2-cm) diameter, optional

Envelope, 3 7/8 by 5 3/8 inches (9.8 by 13.7 cm), or Envelope E pattern, page 89, and instructions, pages 86 to 87, for note card

CROSS CARDS

The cross, the most significant symbol of the Christian faith, is the inspiration for this series of greeting cards. One design is woven, one incorporates a variation of a quilt block called "the Lily" at its center, and another is composed of concentric crosses. Use these designs to convey your best wishes for weddings, baptisms, ordinations, confirmations, and Easter, or to express your sympathy at a time of loss. The cards look best when cut in subtle pastel colors. It's important to photocopy the patterns, rather than tracing them, to ensure accuracy.

♥

WOVEN CROSS CARD

1   Photocopy the patterns, rough cut them out, and set them aside.

2   From the colored paper square cut a 5 1/4- by 7 1/2-inch (13.3- by 19.0-cm) rectangle, reserving the remaining paper for the weaving strips. Score and fold the large rectangle in half crosswise to make a 3 3/4- by 5 1/4-inch (9.5- by 13.3-cm) card.

3   Cut the reserved colored paper in half crosswise. Tape one piece on your cutting mat. Save the remaining piece for another use. Tape the cutting guide pattern for the weaving strips on top of the paper on the cutting mat. Using a craft knife and a straightedge, cut right through the pattern, making weaving strips to match those on the cutting guide. Set the strips aside.

4   Tape the white paper onto the cutting mat. Tape the overlay pattern on top of the white paper. Cut right through the pattern to make six vertical slots in the overlay. Also cut around the edges. Referring to the pattern, lightly mark the numbers on the overlay slots.

5   Note that the numbers on the weaving strips correspond to the numbers on the overlay slots. Working from the back of the overlay, start at the top and weave the strips in numerical order from side to side through the slots. Always working on the back of the overlay, push each woven strip into alignment with its neighbor. Sometimes this can be done best by gently grasping and alternately pulling on each end of the strip as you slide and "walk" it into position.

6   Align and tape the ends of all the strips on the back of the overlay. Spread glue on the back of the overlay and center it on the folded card.

LILY CROSS or CONCENTRIC CROSSES CARD

1   Make three copies of either pattern. To make the full card pattern, precisely cut out the panel pattern from each of the three photocopies. Label one panel A, one panel B, and one panel C. Cut one additional 3 3/4- by 5 1/4-inch (9.5- by 13.3-cm) piece of scrap paper to make a pattern for panel D. Referring to drawing 1, at right, tape the panels together side by side, in ABCD order.

MATERIALS

For one 3 3/4- by 5 1/4-inch (9.5- by 13.3-cm) card

Patterns on pages 94 and 95

7 1/2-inch (19.0-cm) square piece of sturdy colored paper for card and weaving strips (Woven Cross Card)

4- by 5 1/2-inch (10.2- by 14.0-cm) piece of sturdy white paper for overlay (Woven Cross Card)

5 1/4- by 15-inch (13.3- by 38.1-cm) piece of paper (Lily Cross or Concentric Crosses Card)

Envelope, 3 7/8 by 5 3/8 inches (9.8 by 13.7 cm), or Envelope E pattern, page 89, and instructions, pages 86 to 87

NOTE: Duplex paper is a good choice for the Lily Cross or Concentric Crosses Cards, but it isn't required.

2 Referring to drawing 2, use a pencil or marker to add color to the outlined portion of the motifs on each panel.

3 Accordion-fold the patterns into the card format. Hold the folded pattern against a lighted window to check the alignment of the edges and the design motifs on each panel. If the card edges or the design motifs don't align, make adjustments.

4 Tape the card paper to your work surface so that the inside surface of the card faces up. With panel A on the left, tape the pattern in place on top of the card paper. Cutting directly through the pattern and the card paper, cut out the design motifs on panels A, B, and C as shown on drawing 2. Use tiny pinholes to mark the folding lines between each panel. Remove the pattern. Score the folding lines on the card paper. Remove the tape and accordion-fold the card so panel A is on top.

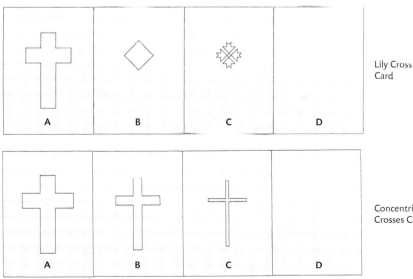

Lily Cross or Concentric Crosses Card

Lily Cross Card

Concentric Crosses Card

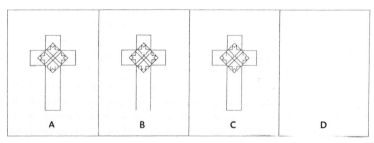

| A | B | C | D |

1. TAPE PHOTOCOPIES TOGETHER TO MAKE COMPLETE PATTERN.

| A | B | C | D |

| A | B | C | D |

2. ADD COLOR TO OUTLINED MOTIF ON EACH PANEL TO INDICATE CUTTING AREA.

SPRINGTIME HATS AND BOXES

This versatile pattern will enable you to make a wardrobe of tiny wearable hats, as well as a variety of small boxes that look just like little hats. The interior box area measures only 2 by 2 $\frac{3}{8}$ by 1 inches (5.1 by 6.0 by 2.5 cm), so think small when you select a gift to put inside.

♥

HAT BOX

1 Photocopy or trace the patterns and roughly cut them out. Pierce the matching dots on the patterns. For the greatest accuracy, attach the patterns to the chosen papers and then cut out the pieces right through the patterns. If you prefer to use the same patterns repeatedly, glue them to acetate before cutting them out.

MATERIALS

For one 3 $\frac{3}{4}$- by 4 $\frac{1}{8}$- by 1 $\frac{1}{4}$-inch (9.5- by 10.5- by 3.2-cm) short hat or box; or one 3 $\frac{3}{4}$- by 4 $\frac{1}{8}$- by 2 $\frac{1}{2}$-inch (9.5- by 10.5- by 6.4-cm) tall hat or box

Patterns on pages 96 and 97

2- by 8-inch (5.1- by 20.3-cm) piece of sturdy paper for short crown, or 3 $\frac{1}{4}$- by 8-inch (8.3- by 20.3-cm) piece of sturdy paper for tall crown

4 $\frac{1}{2}$- by 8 $\frac{1}{2}$-inch (11.4- by 21.6-cm) piece of sturdy paper for brims

1 $\frac{3}{4}$- by 7 $\frac{3}{4}$-inch (4.5- by 19.7-cm) piece of sturdy paper for interior strip

1 $\frac{1}{4}$- by 8-inch (3.2- by 20.3-cm) piece of paper for hatband without bow, or 2 $\frac{1}{4}$- by 8-inch (5.7- by 20.3-cm) piece of paper for hatband, bow, and streamer pieces

Decorative edge scissors for trimming the brim, optional

2 Use a sharp pencil to draw around the patterns and to transfer all the pattern markings. Cut one short or one tall crown. Also cut one hat top, one interior strip, and one of the two hatbands. Cut two brims, but only cut out the center oval of one of the brim pieces and not the other. If you plan to make a scalloped or zigzag edge around the brim, leave a $\frac{1}{8}$-inch (0.3-cm) margin beyond the pencil outline, but do not trim the edge of the brim at this time. If you wish to add a bow to the hatband, also cut out one bow, one bow knot, and one streamer piece.

3 On the right side of the paper, lightly score and fold the broken line near the "tooth" edge of the crown piece. On the right side of the paper, apply glue along the side edge glue tab on the crown piece, overlap it with the opposite side edge to make a tube, and allow it to dry. Working quickly, spread glue in a $\frac{1}{4}$-inch (0.6-cm) border around the reverse side of the hat top piece and apply glue to the "teeth" on the right side of the paper on the crown piece. Matching the dots on both the crown tube and the hat top, join the two pieces together, pressing the teeth of the crown against the reverse side of the hat top. Use removable tape to temporarily hold the pieces together. Place the hat top upside down on your work surface and press the eraser end of a pencil against the glued teeth inside the crown.

4 On the lower edge of the crown, glue the hatband in place. If you are making the hatband with the bow, score the broken lines on the bow knot piece. If you are making a soft bow, score and fold only the four short vertical lines on the bow piece; if you are making a flat bow, score and fold all the vertical lines. Bring the short cut ends of the bow to the shaded center of the piece and glue them there, butting the ends together. Glue the streamer piece behind the bow. Wrap the knot piece around the bow and glue the ends. When dry, glue the bow on the hatband.

5 On the reverse side of the paper, lightly score and fold the broken line near the "tooth" edge of the interior strip. Working quickly, spread glue in a 1/4-inch (0.6-cm) border around the open center on the reverse side of one brim piece and apply glue to the "teeth" on the right side of the interior strip. Match the dots on both the interior strip and the reverse side of the brim piece. Use removable tape to temporarily hold the pieces together. Glue the overlapped glue tab area of the interior strip. Remove the tape. Apply glue to the reverse side of the brim and press the remaining brim piece to the bottom of the hat, aligning the edges and trimming them to match. Use the decorative edge scissors if you wish. The crevice of the scallop or zigzag cut should just touch the pattern line.

WEARABLE HAT

1 Complete step 1 of the instructions for the box, above.

2 Complete step 2 of the instructions, but cut the oval opening in both of the brim pieces.

3 Complete steps 3 and 4 of the instructions.

4 Complete step 5 of the instructions using both open brims so the hat will be wearable. Glue the interior strip to the inside of the crown.

FOLDED FLOWER CARD

Once the warmth and the beauty of the winter holidays have passed, and all of the trimmings have been packed away, I need flowers! We fill our sunroom with potted plants, especially crayon-bright primroses and gerbera daisies, and our breakfast table is pushed against a wall of windows, so we can watch the progress of the daffodils, cresting the surface of the frosty soil. This card would make a charming invitation for an engagement party, a bridal shower, or a small informal wedding.

♥

1   Trace or photocopy the patterns and cut them out. Cut the flower petals to the broken line of the flower center. Pierce the folding lines on both patterns in several places with a pin.

2   Hold the card pattern in place on the paper with removable tape or paper clips. Draw around the outside edge and transfer the folding lines by placing a sharp pencil into the pinholes. Remove the pattern. Connect the folding line dots with very light pencil lines. On the right side of the card, score the two straight folding lines nearest to the curved edges. On the reverse side of the card, score the two folding lines nearest to the center of the card. Flip the card over to the right side of the paper. Make valley folds on both center folding lines. Make mountain folds on the remaining two straight lines near the curved edges.

3   Fold the flower paper square in half and refer back to step 2 to draw and cut two flower sections at once. There is no need to place the pattern on the fold of the paper. On the reverse side of the flower sections, draw and score the curved lines.

4   On the right side of the paper, place glue on each flower section within the flower center area. Place a flower section behind each curved panel of the card. The curved panels will become the flower center when the card is closed.

MATERIALS

For one 4-inch (10.2-cm) diameter card

Patterns on page 97

2 1/2- by 7-inch (6.4- by 17.8-cm) piece of paper for card

5-inch (12.7-cm) square of paper for flower

Envelope, 4 1/4 by 5 1/8 inches (10.8 by 13.0 cm), or Envelope C pattern, page 88, and instructions, pages 86 to 87

SPRING NAPKIN RINGS

Three favorite springtime symbols—a heart, a flower, and a butterfly—embellish these napkin ring designs. To change the circumference of the rings, adjust the pattern by lengthening or shortening the band that runs between the two split motifs.

♥

1 Photocopy or trace the napkin ring pattern of your choice. Glue the pattern to acetate, if you wish, and cut it out.

2 Attach the pattern to the paper with removable tape or paper clips and trace completely around the pattern shape. Transfer the slot lines at each end of the ring. Using a craft knife and a straightedge on a protected work surface, cut out the shape and slice each slot line. On the butterfly, score along the body center line and each wing line. On the flower, score around the center area and cut between the petals.

3 Referring to the drawing below, bring the ends of the ring together, interlocking the slots of the heart, flower, or butterfly sections so a complete motif is formed on the outside of the ring at the center front. On the butterfly, make a mountain fold at the body center and a valley fold along each wing, and curl the antennae to the front. On the flower, glue the center in place and lift and fold the petals forward and around it.

MATERIALS

For one 1³/₄ inch (4.4-cm) diameter napkin ring

Patterns on page 98

2¹/₂- by 8-inch (6.4- by 20.3-cm) piece of sturdy paper

1-inch (2.5-cm) circle of paper for flower center

Round toothpick for curling butterfly antennae

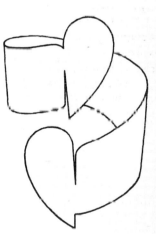

CURL AND INTERLOCK
THE RING.

CHAPTER THREE

SUMMER FESTIVITIES

Here comes summer! It's playtime again with parades and parties, dozy days at the beach, and noisy nights under firecracker skies. Hang the flag, pack a picnic, pull up a hammock, and count the clouds. This chapter uses playful symbols of the season, like pinwheels, stars, T-shirts, and lemonade to make paper projects for special occasions or just for fun. Grab your workbox, find a shady spot, and make something!

LEMONADE CARD

A big frosty glass of lemonade is a refreshing greeting for summer celebrations. Use a white pen or pencil to inscribe your good wishes inside the card. This design fits inside a standard business envelope, but to create something more festive, unfold a standard envelope and use it as a pattern on your own pretty paper.

MATERIALS

For one 3 3/4- by 9-inch (9.5- by 22.9-cm) card

Patterns on page 99

8 1/2- by 11-inch (21.6- by 28.0-cm) piece of plain or patterned sheer vellum for glass

6-inch (15.2-cm) square of yellow glassine paper or sheer vellum for lemonade

2-inch (5.1-cm) square of pale yellow paper for lemon sections

2 1/4-inch (5.7-cm) square of white paper for lemon pith

2 1/2-inch (6.4-cm) square of bright yellow paper for rind

1- by 8 7/8-inch (2.5- by 22.5-cm) piece of diagonally cut striped paper for straw

White pen or sharp white pencil

Envelope, 4 1/8 by 9 1/2 inches (10.5 by 24.1 cm)

1 Trace or photocopy the patterns. Pierce the placement lines in a few places. Cut out the patterns.

2 Score and fold the glass paper in half to make a 5 1/2- by 8 1/2-inch (14.0- by 21.6-cm) piece. Unfold the paper and fold each short edge to the center folding line leaving a hairline between the two edges. Refold the paper to make a 2 3/4- by 8 1/2-inch (7.0- by 21.6-cm) card, with two vertical pockets inside.

3 Tape or clip the glass pattern on the folded paper so that the top and side edges align. Draw the bottom edge of the glass on the paper and remove the pattern. Tape or clip together the folded paper edges and cut out the glass shape.

4 Score and fold the lemonade paper to make a 3- by 6-inch (7.6- by 15.2-cm) piece. Place the lemonade pattern on top and tape or clip the layers together. Draw around the pattern and remove it, leaving the tape or clips in place. Cut out the pieces. Unfold the glass-shaped card and slide a lemonade piece inside each pocket, placing them in their proper positions and temporarily anchoring them with removable tape. Leave the card unfolded.

5 Score and fold the striped paper to make a 1/2- by 8 7/8-inch (1.3- by 22.5-cm) piece. Place glue inside the folded paper and press it together until it is dry. Trim the unfolded edge to make a 1/4- by 8 7/8-inch (0.6- by 22.5-cm) straw. Slide it inside the left pocket of the unfolded card so it rests underneath the inside glass layer and on top of the lemonade. Refold the card. When you look at the card front, the straw should rest behind the lemonade. Unfold the left pocket and glue the straw to the lemonade. Then place a little glue on the straw and refold the left pocket so that the straw will also stick to the glass paper layer inside the card.

6 Unfold the right pocket of the card and add a dot of glue to the reverse side of the lemonade. Refold the right pocket as well as the card, making sure that the lemonade layers align when the card is folded.

7 Cut one bright yellow rind piece, one white pith piece, and one pale yellow lemon piece. Center and glue one upon the other. Use a white pen or pencil to draw the lemon sections. Slide the slot of the slice over the rim of the glass. Add a tiny glue dot under the portion of the slice that overlaps the card front.

FRUIT BASKETS

Delectable fruit slices inspired these little summer party baskets. Fill them up with fruit-flavored gumdrops or jelly beans or use one to hold a present or a gift certificate.

✳

1 Trace the basket pattern, transferring the markings. Observe the arrows at the center bottom of the basket pattern and cut as directed. Trace either the watermelon slice or the citrus section pattern and cut it out. Trace the rind piece with the folding lines on folded tracing paper and cut it out.

2 Tape or clip the basket pattern onto the white paper. Draw one basket, transfer the markings, and cut out the piece. Cut into the areas at the center bottom of the basket to the points indicated on the pattern. On each long edge of the basket center strip, score and fold the straight lines across the base of the fruit slices and the base of the glue tabs. Score and fold the two parallel lines at the center bottom of the basket.

3 Draw and cut out two watermelon slices or eight citrus sections for each basket. Referring to the photograph, glue one watermelon slice or four citrus sections in place on each side of the basket. Use the paper punch to cut black seed dots for the watermelon and glue them in place.

4 Assemble the basket, forming the base and the sides by gluing the tabs along the edges of the center strip to the inside of the fruit slices. Trim the glue tabs slightly if they show above the top straight edges of the basket. To form the handle, butt together, but do not overlap, the ends of the strip at the center top of the basket and place transparent tape over and under the handle in this area. Cut one rind piece, scoring and folding the ends as indicated on the pattern. Cut this as one smooth piece with no fold at the center top. Glue the rind on top of the center strip of the basket, starting at the center bottom, covering the butted and taped edges of the handle at the center top, and finishing at the center bottom.

MATERIALS

For one 3³/₈-inch (8.6-cm) diameter basket

Patterns on page 100

4¹/₂- by 11-inch (11.4- by 27.9 cm) piece of sturdy white paper

3¹/₂-inch (8.9-cm) square of red paper for watermelon or pastel citrus-colored paper for citrus fruit

1¹/₈- by 11-inch (2.8- by 27.9-cm) piece of green paper for watermelon rind or bright citrus-colored paper for citrus fruit rind

Scrap of black paper and paper punch, ¹/₈" (0.3 cm) diameter, for watermelon seeds

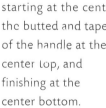

GARDEN GLOVES GIFT CARD

MATERIALS

For one 3 7/8- by 8 5/8-inch (9.8- by 21.9-cm) card

Patterns on page 101

9- by 12-inch (22.9- by 30.5-cm) piece of sturdy canvas-colored paper for gloves

Two 3 1/4- by 4 1/4-inch (8.3- by 10.8-cm) pieces of blue paper for cuffs

Envelope, 4 1/8 by 9 1/2 inches (10.5 by 24.1 cm)

Tuck a small flat gift such as a packet of seeds or tickets to a garden show inside the thumb pocket of these work gloves. Unfold a standard business-size envelope and use it as a pattern to make a unique custom envelope for the card. Place the thumb edge of the card in the envelope first, so when the card is pulled out, nothing will be accidentally left inside the envelope. You also may wish to secure the gift item with a piece of removable tape placed under the thumb on the card front.

✳

1 Photocopy or trace the patterns and cut them out, making sure to cut into the slots between the fingers.

2 Score and fold the glove paper in half crosswise to make a 6- by 9-inch (15.2- by 22.9-cm) unit. Align the "place on fold" edge of the glove pattern with the folded edge of the glove paper. Hold the pieces together with paper clips or removable tape. Trace around the pattern and mark the cuts between the fingers. Remove the pattern but leave the tape, or clips, in place to hold the paper layers together.

3 Using a craft knife on a protected surface, cut out the glove. Cut the slots between the fingers, including the thumb and the pinky. Remove the tape, or clips, unfold the card so the inside surface faces up, and score the thumb folding lines. Fold one thumb toward the outside surface of the card front and glue the lower edge in place. Fold the other thumb toward the outside surface of the card back and glue the lower edge in place.

4 Score and fold each piece of blue paper in half crosswise to make two 2 1/8- by 3 1/4-inch (5.4- by 8.3-cm) folded pieces. Align the "place on fold" edge of the cuff pattern on the folded edge of each blue paper. Trace around the pattern, remove it, and cut out the cuffs. Glue one cuff in place on the card front, sandwiching the bottom edge of the front glove within the folded cuff piece. Use the remaining half piece to finish the lower edge of the glove on the card back.

CLASSIC SUMMER TOTE

Gardening, picnicking, boating, beachcombing—just the sight of this canvas carryall evokes nostalgic memories of summertime fun. This is an easy project, but it does require some time and patience. For best results, the grain of the paper should run parallel to the longest edges of each piece of paper.

❊

1   Photocopy or trace the pattern pieces and cut them out. Pierce the patterns along the placement folding lines.

2   Cut one 1- by 8 1/2-inch (2.5- by 21.6-cm) strip from each piece of paper and glue the two pieces together. When the unit is dry, cut two handles, each 5/16 by 8 1/4 inches (0.7 by 21 cm). Curl the handles slightly by pulling the canvas-colored side along a scissor blade.

3   Place the bag pattern on the canvas-colored paper and trace around the shape. Transfer all of the placement lines and folding lines with a sharp pencil.

4   Cut out the bag. Connect the dots to draw the placement and folding lines. On the reverse side score the folding line along each top edge. Fold the top edges toward the right side of the bag, creasing them sharply and gluing them in place. Use removable tape or clips to flatten the glued areas.

5   Referring to the drawing, spread glue within the shaded parallel handle areas on the right side of the bag. Add the handles and anchor them with removable tape or clips to keep them aligned as you complete the bag.

6   On the right side of the bag, spread glue along the two shaded side edges. Without making any sharp folds, curl the bag piece somewhat, lifting the top folded edges toward each other as you overlap and press one set of side edges together. Again hold the piece together with tape or clips. Overlap and glue together the remaining side edges and allow to dry.

7   To close each side of the bag bottom, gently press the base up to one side until the dot on the base aligns with the "side seam" of the bag. Butt the edges together and use traditional transparent tape on the outside of the bag to close the openings. Push in each pointed corner of the bag just a tiny bit.

8   From the colored paper, cut one base overlay. Transfer the folding and cutting lines with a sharp pencil.

9   Cut out the base overlay. Connect the pencil dots to draw the folding and cutting lines. Cut into the overlay as indicated on the pattern. On the reverse side of the paper, reinforce the end of each cut with a piece of tape.

10 Score and crease the diagonal folding lines on the right side of the overlay. Lift and bring together the short cut edges. Align the dots, and butt and tape the edges together. Spread glue around the inside edges of the overlay. Place the bag inside the overlay. Fold up the pointed flaps and glue them in place. Use removable tape to hold everything together until dry.

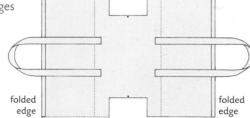

folded edge   folded edge

GLUE HANDLES IN PLACE ON BAG.

MATERIALS

For one 3 3/4- by 2 5/8- by 1 1/2-inch (9.5- by 6.7- by 3.8-cm) bag

Patterns on page 102

6 3/4- by 8 1/2-Inch (17.1- by 21.6-cm) canvas-colored piece of paper for bag and handles

4 1/4- by 8 1/2-inch (10.8- by 21.6-cm) colored piece of paper for handles and base overlay

PARTY HAT

What could be easier to make than a playful party hat? This classic chapeau can be cut from a variety of sturdy papers including the sample pages of a discontinued wallpaper book. Add stickers, feathers, fringes, streamers, and other imaginative trimmings to customize your creation. How stunning!

❁

1 Select the small or the large hat pattern. Fold a piece of tracing paper in half, place the folded edge of the tracing paper on the pattern's center front line and trace the pattern. After taping or clipping the tracing paper edges together, cut out the hat pattern and unfold it. It will resemble the drawing below.

2 Tape or clip the unfolded pattern on the reverse side of the party hat paper. Draw around the shape, transferring all of the markings. Cut out the shape. On the right side of the paper, transfer one back overlap line as pictured on the drawing and lightly score the reinforcement tabs along the curved edge. Fold the reinforcement tabs to the reverse side of the hat and glue them in place there. Punch holes where they are indicated on the tabs.

3 On the reverse side of the hat, glue or tape one end of each paper strip around the top opening of the hat, but do not place the paper strips within the overlap areas. If you wish, trim or curl the free ends of the strips. To create a pom-pom effect, cut six 6-inch (15.2-cm) lengths of 1/8-inch (0.3-cm) wide paper and tape together the ends of each separate piece before attaching to the hat.

4 Apply glue to the back overlap area that has been marked on the right side of the paper. Form a cone by bringing the opposite unglued overlap area around to cover the glued area. Allow the glue to dry.

5 Knot one end of the elastic cord. Placing the knot inside the hat, thread the cut end of the elastic out through the hole. Bring the elastic around to the opposite hole, thread it through the hole and knot it inside the hat. The elastic may seem very long, but the length is easily adjusted for comfort after trying on the hat. Just re-knot the elastic inside the hat.

MATERIALS

For one large (adult) 7-inch (17.8-cm) hat; or one small (child) 5 3/4-inch (14.6-cm) hat

Pattern on page 103

12-inch (30.5-cm) square of sturdy paper for large hat; 10-inch (25.4-cm) square for small hat

Six long pieces of 1/8-inch (0.3-cm) wide paper, such as quilling strips, for trimming

22-inch (55.9-cm) length of round cord elastic for large hat; 18-inch (45.7-cm) length for small hat

DRAW HALF PATTERN ON FOLDED TRACING PAPER TO MAKE COMPLETE HAT PATTERN.

SIMPLE STAR

Hung as an ornament, taped on a gift box, placed as a favor, or pinned to a bulletin board, this star is perfect for lots of stellar occasions. For Fourth of July festivities red, white, and blue is the palette of choice, of course, but the stars will really sparkle at Christmastime too when cut from brilliant foil papers. At Halloween, enlarge and reduce the pattern for variety and use glow-in-the-dark paper for a spooktacular effect! To make the Uncle Sam hat shown here, follow the instructions for the Springtime Hats and Boxes on pages 34 and 35, using the tall crown pattern instead of the short one.

MATERIALS

For one 5 1/4-inch (13.3-cm) diameter star

Pattern on page 104

6 1/2-inch (16.5-cm) square of medium-weight paper

10-inch (25.4-cm) length of monofilament

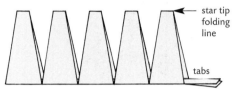

star tip folding line

tabs

FOLD PIECE IN HALF ALONG STAR TIP FOLDING LINE. OVERLAP ONE GLUE-COVERED SHADED AREA WITH OTHER SHADED AREA.

1 Trace or photocopy the pattern and glue it to acetate if you wish. Cut out the pattern. Pierce the folding lines in a few places.

2 Tape or clip the pattern in place on the paper. Stripes look best when they are parallel to the star tip folding line labeled on the pattern. Use a sharp pencil to trace around the outside edge of the pattern and within the cut out areas. Transfer the folding lines by placing a pencil in the pinholes.

3 Cut out the piece. Score all of the M (mountain) folding lines on the front. Flip the piece over to the reverse side and score all of the V (valley) folding lines

4 Flip the piece back to the right side. Crease all of the M folding lines, making mountain folds. Crease all of the V folding lines making valley folds.

5 On the right side of the paper, spread glue along one of the shaded areas, avoiding the tab. Fold the piece in half along the star tip folding line. Overlap the glue-covered shaded area with the other shaded area to create the core of the star. The tabs should not be glued together. The unit will resemble the drawing above right.

6 Spread apart the two tabs at one end of the core area. Place glue on the inside surface of both tabs, but do not stick them together. Holding the tabs in one hand and the opposite end of the core in the other hand, form a doughnut, bringing the ends of the core together and overlapping them as you place one glue tab inside the core and the other tab outside the core. Thread the piece of monofilament through one star tip and tie the ends in a knot.

TWIN POP NOTES

Use these frosty symbols of summer to send sweet notes and party invitations. Can't you almost hear the bells and music of the ice cream truck?

❄

1   Photocopy or trace the patterns and cut them out.

2   Score and fold the beige paper in half. Place the complete ice cream bar pattern on the fold and hold it in place with removable tape or paper clips. Draw around the shape and remove the pattern. Replace the clips or tape and cut out the shape using a craft knife on a protected surface. Fold the colored paper squares in half. Place the overlay pattern on each folded square and trace around it, holding the edges of each folded square together with tape or paper clips. Cut out each shape to make four pop overlays.

3   On the outside of the card, front and back, glue two of the pop overlay pieces. Glue the remaining pop overlay pieces inside the card after slightly trimming each piece along the straight edge that will rest next to the center folding line. If necessary, trim the edges to match.

4   If you wish, use a stylus or dull knife to lightly score the dotted vertical line on each surface of the card. Then fold the card somewhat on each line to give it a little dimension. To give the twin pop a slightly rounded appearance, use a large glue stick tube or something of similar size to roll each "twin" vertically inside the card.

MATERIALS

*For one 2 ³/₄- by 6 ¹/₈-inch
(7.0- by 15.6-cm) note card*

Patterns on page 105

6 ¹/₂-inch (16.5-cm) square of sturdy beige paper

Two 6-inch (15.2-cm) squares of lightweight fruit-colored paper

Envelope, 3 ⁵/₈ by 6 ¹/₂ inches (9.2 by 16.5 cm), or Envelope D pattern, page 89, and instructions, pages 86 to 87

PIGS AND PIGLETS

Mix bright floral and geometric prints to create a colorful family of paper pigs and piglets. The back sides are left open so these little piggies can carry rolled-up money, gift certificates, tickets, invitations, or very small and lightweight presents.

❀

1 Trace or photocopy the patterns, transferring all of the markings. Cut out the patterns. Use a paper punch to make holes for the eyes and nostrils. Cut slots for the ears.

2 Attach the patterns to the right side of the paper with removable tape. Draw one body, one underbody, and two ears. Transfer the markings for the curved ear slots, eyes, nostrils, and folding lines onto the right side of the body. It isn't necessary to transfer the dotted lines indicating the placement of the glue tabs on the body. On the right side of the ears, transfer the curved line above the glue tabs. On the right side of the underbody, transfer all of the folding lines.

3 Remove the patterns and cut out the pieces. With the right side of the paper always facing up, lightly score each folding line on all of the pieces. On the body piece, cut the ear slots and use a paper punch to make the eyes and nostrils. On the ears, score the curved line near the glue tabs.

4 Gently curve the body of the pig, coaxing it into an arch. Curl the tail and ears by carefully pulling them over a scissor blade or rolling them around a straw or a dowel. Place glue on the ear glue tabs and slide the tabs into the ear slot on the body piece. Working inside the body, with the help of tweezers, if necessary, separate the glue tabs somewhat and press them against the reverse side of the body piece. Refer to the body pattern to see the approximate placement of the ear glue tabs.

5 Fold up the glue tabs on the underbody and apply glue to the right side of the tabs. Referring to the body pattern for placement, align the underbody along one side of the pig starting at the mouth. When this side is dry, glue the other side in place. Fold the nose and glue tabs on the scored lines, apply glue to the right side of the tabs, and set the nose in place. Use a dowel or the eraser end of a pencil to press the tabs against the reverse side of the body.

MATERIALS

For one large pig, 3 7/8 inches (9.8 cm) long, or one small piglet, 1 15/16 inches (4.9 cm) long

Patterns on page 106

6- by 10-inch (15.2- by 25.4-cm) piece of plain or patterned paper for pig

4- by 6-inch (10.2- by 15.2-cm) piece of plain or patterned paper for piglet

Paper punch, 1/8-inch (0.3-cm) diameter for pig, 1/16-inch (0.2-cm) diameter for piglet

NOTE: *If you don't have paper punches of the correct size, use a craft knife or large needle to make the tiny holes.*

GIFT TAG AND PARTY BAG

Make a simple statement with basic stenciled letters on a traditional tag shape. There is room enough to add the "to" and "from" names above and below the line of cut-out letters. When making the companion party bag, select brilliantly colored duplex paper to add extra zing to the project.

STENCIL GIFT TAG

1   Photocopy the gift tag pattern or trace it, but do not cut it out. Glue the pattern to the acetate and allow it to dry. Cut out the letters to make a stencil and then cut out the tag shape.

2   Tape or clip the pattern to the paper. Trace inside the letters and around the tag. Remove the pattern and cut out the letters, and then the tag. Attach the string.

PARTY BAG

To make the 5 1/4- by 6 1/8- by 2 5/8-inch (13.3- by 15.5- by 6.7-cm) party bag, first make a 175-percent photocopy enlargement of the Mini Shopping Bag pattern on page 120. Trim away 1/4 inch (0.6 cm) of the glue tab on the enlarged pattern to make it 1/2 inch (1.3 cm). Place the pattern on a 12- by 17-inch (30.5- by 43.2-cm) piece of bond-weight duplex paper. Also cut two handles, each 1/2 by 7 1/4 inches (1.3 by 18.4 cm), but do not fold them. To complete the party bag, refer to the instructions and drawings for the Mini Shopping Bag on page 78.

MATERIALS

For one 2 1/8- by 3 5/8-inch (5.4- by 9.2-cm) tag

Pattern on page 104

2 1/2- by 4-inch (6.4- by 10.2-cm) piece of acetate

2 1/2- by 4-inch (6.4- by 10.2-cm) piece of sturdy paper

Cord or string

PINWHEEL NAPKIN RINGS

Perky pinwheel napkin rings are quick to make and they can double as place cards at festive occasions. To add pizzazz, use duplex paper or two unglued layers of lightweight paper in contrasting colors.

❄

1 Photocopy or trace the patterns. Glue the uncut patterns to a piece of acetate if you wish. Cut out the patterns and punch out the dots.

2 Use removable tape or paper clips to attach the pinwheel and ring patterns to the paper. If using two coordinating papers instead of duplex paper, stack one paper on the other and join them together with removable tape. Do not glue the paper layers together. Cut out the shapes.

3 On the pinwheel piece, cut into the slots that define each blade without cutting and distorting the blade tips. Punch out all of the dots. Cut out the dot at the center of the pinwheel by hand if your paper punch can't reach it. If the paper is somewhat heavy, gently pull each blade over a scissor edge to curl it. Also curl the rings in the same way.

4 Push the shank of the brad fastener through the hole of each pinwheel blade in succession. Then push the shank through the hole at the center of the pinwheel. Finally, push the shank through the single hole on the ring piece and then through one of the remaining holes on the ring.
Open the arms of the shank.

MATERIALS

For one 1³/₄ inch (4.4-cm) diameter napkin ring

Patterns on page 105

One 5- by 7-inch (12.7- by 17.8-cm) piece of duplex paper or two 5- by 7-inch (12.7- by 17.8-cm) pieces of lightweight contrasting paper

Brad fastener with ³/₄-inch (1.9-cm) shank

Paper punch, ¹/₈-inch (0.3-cm) diameter

SUMMER TEE SET

T-shirts and shorts, those ubiquitous symbols of summer fun, make playful motifs for seasonal stationery. These simple designs are very quick and easy to make and they look best when made with a mix of bright patterns and stripes. Send the T-shirt by itself or use the two pieces together in the same envelope when you want to add just one more "short" note!

T-SHIRT CARD

1   Photocopy or trace the patterns with the markings and cut them out. Pierce all of the folding lines and the placement lines in several places with a pin.

2   To make the shirt, tape or clip the shirt and sleeve patterns on the right side of the striped paper. Draw around the outside edges of the patterns. Use a pencil point placed in the pinholes to transfer the folding lines.

3   Remove the patterns and cut out the two pieces, including the neck openings. On the striped side of the paper on both pieces, score all of the folding lines except the diagonal lines on

FOLD SLEEVE PIECE AS SHOWN.

MATERIALS

For one shirt, 5 3/4 by 4 1/8 inches (14.6 by 10.5 cm), and one pair of shorts, 4 1/2 by 3 1/8 inches (11.4 by 7.9 cm)

Patterns on page 107

6 1/2- by 9-inch (16.5- by 22.9-cm) piece of striped paper for the shirt, stripes parallel to the short edge

6- by 8-inch (15.2- by 20.3-cm) piece of patterned paper for the shorts

Paper crimper, optional

Envelope 4 3/8 by 5 3/8 inches (11.1 by 14.6 cm), or Envelope B pattern, page 88, and instructions, pages 86 to 87

the sleeve piece. Flip the sleeve piece over to the reverse side. Hold the sleeve pattern against the reverse side of the paper and transfer the diagonal folding lines. Remove the pattern and score those diagonal lines. Flip the sleeve piece over to the striped side again.

4 On both pieces, make all mountain folds except for the diagonal folding lines on the sleeve piece; those lines should be valley folds. Work with the folding lines of the sleeve piece to create a unit resembling the drawing at left. Spread glue within the shaded area on the striped side of the folded sleeve piece. Unfold the shirt and place the folded sleeve piece on top of it, aligning the two pieces along the neck edges and all of the folded common edges. Fold down the shirt front to overlap the sleeve piece. Before the glue dries, unfold the unit to be sure that it will open completely and refold. If the neck edges don't align precisely, trim them to match when the glue is dry.

SHORT NOTE

To make the shorts, first cut off a 1- by 7-inch (2.5- by 17.8-cm) piece of the patterned paper and reserve it for the waistband. Score and fold the remaining patterned paper in half crosswise to make a 5- by 3 1/2 inch (12.7- by 8.9-cm) folded piece. Align the "place on fold" edge of the shorts pattern with the folded edge of the patterned paper, trace around the outside edge and cut out the shorts. Unfold the shorts and hold the pattern against the reverse side to transfer the waistband folding lines. Still working on the reverse side, score these two folding lines and crease them with mountain folds. Place glue between the two folding lines (on the shaded area of the pattern) and refold the shorts so the waistband area will be joined. From the reserved piece of the patterned paper, cut one waistband. On the right side of the paper, score and mountain fold the folding lines. Glue the waistband in place. To make a textured waistband, cut a 1/2- by 7-inch (1.3- by 17.8-cm) piece of paper from the reserved strip of paper and crimp it, following the crimper manufacturer's instructions. Trim it to fit and glue it in place.

CHAPTER FOUR

AUTUMN TRADITIONS

The changing light and chilly nights of autumn inspire our thanks for the last gifts of the garden and anticipation of the cozy pleasures to come. Filled to the brim with themes and schemes to celebrate the season, this chapter is a harvest of ideas for hearth and home, family and friends. Witches' hats, spooky bats, friendly ghosts, and piles of pumpkins all hide in scraps of paper, waiting for your hands to find them.

LEAF GARLAND AND WREATH

If you believe that it is impossible to do two things at once, this project just might change your mind! Using one basic pattern, cut a collection of folded leaves from autumn-hued papers and link them together to create a garland. Then, take the leaf shapes cut from the center of each link and cluster them together on a ring of paper to make a petite leaf wreath.

MATERIALS

For one 40-inch (101.6-cm) garland

Pattern on page 108

4-inch (10.2-cm) square of acetate

Fourteen 3³/₄- by 7¹/₂-inch (9.5- by 19.1-cm) pieces of paper in various autumn colors

GARLAND

1 Photocopy or trace the pattern and glue it to acetate. Cut out the leaf and the leaf center, reserving both pieces.

2 Score and fold each piece of paper in half crosswise to make a 3³/₄-inch (9.5-cm) square. Align the "place on fold" edge of the pattern along the folded edge of each piece of paper. Holding the layers together with removable tape or paper clips, trace around the outside and inside of the shape. Remove the pattern, but leave the tape or clips in place.

3 Beginning at the center, cut out the leaf interior and then the exterior shape. Repeat to make twenty links. Reserve all of the small leaves cut from the interior of each link.

4 To link the first two leaves together, first fold link 1, as shown in drawing 1 on the next page. Then, referring to drawing 2, unfold link 2 and gently curl its upper single leaf portion, inserting it through the opening of folded link 1 from front to back. Referring to drawing 3, fold link 2 so that link 1 hangs inside it, enclosing the leaf tip. Continue to link the remaining leaves together in the same way, one by one, from bottom to top.

WREATH

1 Photocopy or trace the patterns. Cut out the base pattern. If you have reserved the center leaf pattern from the garland project, move on to step 2. Otherwise, glue the center of the leaf pattern onto acetate and cut it out.

2 Use a large needle to pierce the center dot on the leaf pattern, as well as the dots on the ends of the two slots on either side of the center line. If you are using the leaves from the garland project, hold the pattern against each leaf, transfer the slot positions with a pencil, and go to step 3. Otherwise, score and fold each piece of paper in half crosswise to make a 3-inch (7.6-cm) square. Holding the layers together with removable tape or paper clips, center the leaf pattern on the folded paper. Trace around the shape and transfer the slot positions with pencil dots. Remove the pattern and cut two leaves at once.

3 Referring to the pattern and starting at each dot, cut three slots at the base of each leaf, one at the center and one on each side of the center slot. Score all of the mountain folding lines (labeled M) on the front of the leaf and score all of the valley folds (labeled V) on the reverse side of the leaf. Crease all of the folding lines.

4 On the base pattern, use a large needle to pierce the central folding line in several places. Also pierce the ends of each slot. On the brown paper draw two wreath base sections, and use a pencil to transfer the placement of the slots and the folding line. Remove the pattern, cut the slots, and score the central folding line on each section. Cut out the wreath base sections. Crease the base sections on the scored lines, creating mountain folds. Overlap and glue the sections together to form a ring.

5 On a flat surface place the leaves in a circle, making a pleasing color arrangement. The two short slots cut at the base of each leaf have created little tabs that can be inserted into the slots on the wreath base. First fit the slot on the innermost circle of the base. No glue is required. Continue to overlap and insert each leaf in place.

MATERIALS

For one 8 1/2-inch (21.6-cm) diameter wreath

Patterns on page 108

3-inch (7.6-cm) square of acetate

Twenty-eight leftover leaves from centers of leaf garland links or fourteen 3- by 6-inch (7.6- by 15.2-cm) pieces of paper in various autumn colors

8- by 9-inch (20.3- by 22.9-cm) piece of sturdy brown paper for base

Monofilament for hanging loop

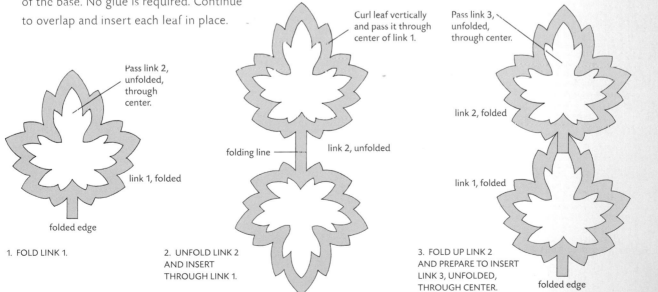

Pass link 2, unfolded, through center.

link 1, folded

folded edge

1. FOLD LINK 1.

Curl leaf vertically and pass it through center of link 1.

folding line — link 2, unfolded

2. UNFOLD LINK 2 AND INSERT THROUGH LINK 1.

Pass link 3, unfolded, through center.

link 2, folded

link 1, folded

3. FOLD UP LINK 2 AND PREPARE TO INSERT LINK 3, UNFOLDED, THROUGH CENTER.

folded edge

SQUIRREL NOTE AND GARLAND

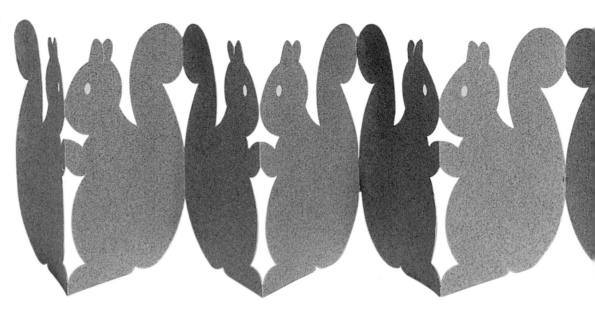

Naughty squirrels are so pesky and brazen, but sometimes they are so cute and funny! The squirrels featured in these projects are some of the players from our backyard team who scrimmage on the roof, leap from the branches, hang on the bird feeder, dig up the bulbs, nibble the seedlings, bite all the peaches, sway on the sunflowers, and remind us daily of the importance of play.

SQUIRREL NOTE

1 Photocopy or trace the note pattern, and cut it out. Use the paper punch to cut out the eye.

2 Score and fold the paper in half crosswise to make a 4- by 5-inch (10.2- by 12.7-cm) note card.

3 Align the "place on fold" edge of the pattern with the folded edge of the card. Hold the pattern in place with removable tape or paper clips. Draw around the shape and within the eye. Remove the pattern.

MATERIALS

For one 3⁷/₈- by 4⁷/₈-inch (9.8- by 12.4-cm) note

Pattern on page 109

5- by 8-inch (12.7- by 20.3-cm) piece of sturdy paper

Paper punch, ³/₁₆- or ¹/₄-inch (0.5- to 0.6-cm) diameter

Envelope, 4¹/₄ by 5¹/₈ inches (10.8 by 13.0 cm), or Envelope C pattern, page 88, and instructions, pages 86 to 87

4 Anchor the folded card layers together with clips. Cut out the squirrel shape and punch out the eye.

SQUIRREL GARLAND

1 Photocopy the squirrel garland pattern, or trace it, and cut it out. Punch out the eye.

2 Fold each 3 1/2- by 9-inch (8.9- by 22.9-cm) piece of paper in half to 3 1/2 by 4 1/2 inches (8.9 by 11.4 cm). Unfold the paper and bring each short edge to meet at the center fold and crease the folds. The paper should have four equal sections divided by folding lines. Unfold the paper and refold it on the same folding lines, making accordion (alternating mountain and valley) folds. Crease all of the folding lines sharply. The folded paper will measure 2 1/4 by 3 1/2 inches (5.7 by 8.9 cm).

3 Place the squirrel pattern on the folded paper. The side edges of the pattern should touch the folded edges of the paper. Tape or clip the pattern in place, draw around the shape, and remove the pattern.

4 Anchor the folded paper layers together with removable tape or paper clips. Using a craft knife on a protected work surface, cut out the squirrel shape.

5 Repeat the process with the remaining pieces of paper to make additional sections of garland. Join the sections together with transparent tape.

MATERIALS

For three garland sections, each 2 7/8 by 9 inches (7.3 by 22.9 cm)

Pattern on page 109

Three 3 1/2- by 9-inch (8.9- by 22.9-cm) pieces of lightweight paper

Paper punch, 1/8-inch (0.3-cm) diameter

NOTE: *If paper does not fold well, it may be necessary to score it before folding.*

CRESCENT MOON ORNAMENT

If you are just beginning to work with paper, there are lots of better places in the book to start! This design is somewhat challenging, so save the moon until you have gained a little more experience.

1 Photocopy the patterns or trace them, transferring all of the markings. Cut out the patterns.

2 Anchor the patterns on the paper with removable tape or paper clips and trace around the shapes, drawing one rim, one profile strip, two stars, one moon, and one moon in reverse. Transfer all of the markings. Using a craft knife and a straightedge on a protected work surface, cut out the pieces. Score the glue tabs and folding lines where indicated on the patterns. Cut out the smile. Punch out the eye. Gently pull the profile strip over the edge of a pair of scissors or a ruler to curl it slightly. Referring to the drawing below, crease the folds of the profile strip on the score lines. Crease the folding lines on all the remaining pieces.

3 Apply glue to the right side of the tabs on one moon. Press the tabs to the reverse side of one edge of the profile strip, referring to the pattern notes for the correct alignment. Hold the tabs in place until dry. Apply glue to the tabs on the remaining moon and attach it to the other edge of the profile strip. Set the piece aside.

4 Glue 1/4 inch (0.6 cm) of the end of the monofilament to the reverse side of one star tip. Glue the remaining star on top, sandwiching the monofilament inside. Allow it to dry. Glue the free end of the monofilament to the X on the top glue tab of the profile strip. Fold the glue tabs at the ends of the profile strip toward the moon. Eventually the tabs will be glued to the rim and hidden by the moon.

5 Glue one end of the ribbon to the X on the end of the rim. Allow it to dry. Loop the ribbon and glue the remaining end on top of the first end. Form the rim into a circle, add glue to the tab, and clip it in place until dry.

6 Before adding glue to the small tabs on the rim, fit the moon unit inside of the rim, aligning the dots at the center top and bottom. Use a strip of scrap paper to push glue onto the tabs at each end of the profile strip. Hold the glue tabs and the rim together until dry. On one side of the ornament, lift the edge of the moon and apply glue to the tabs along the rim. Press the edge of the moon onto the tabs and hold the unit in place until it is dry. Repeat on the other side of the ornament.

MATERIALS

For one 3-inch (7.6-cm) ornament

Patterns on page 110

3 1/2- by 11-inch (8.9- by 27.9-cm) piece of sturdy yellow art paper

Paper punch, 1/8-inch (0.3-cm) diameter

Monofilament

4-inch (10.2-cm) length of narrow yellow ribbon

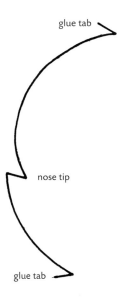

glue tab

nose tip

glue tab

1. FOLD AND CURL PROFILE STRIP.

CURLED STARS

Create your own little galaxy of curled paper stars, using scraps of stationery, origami paper, and foil. For even greater glitter, cut these stellar shapes from glow-in-the-dark paper. Such luminous material tends to be rather expensive, but since each star requires only a 5 1/2-inch (14.0-cm) square of paper, it just may be worth the splurge.

1 Photocopy or trace the pattern and glue it to acetate. Allow the pattern to dry and cut it out, leaving the paper on the acetate. Cut out the small star at the center of the pattern. Pierce all of the dots labeled A1 through A5, B1 through B5, and C1 through C5. Also pierce each single dot at the end of each cutting line near the center star.

2 Use removable tape or paper clips to hold the pattern in place on the right side of the paper. The paper surface facing up will appear inside the star. With a sharp pencil, trace around the pattern and within the star. Push a pencil into each pierced dot to transfer. Remove the pattern. Cut out the pentagon and the star at the center.

3 Referring to drawing 1, make cuts from each corner of the pentagon to the single dot near the center area. When the sides of each segment are curled, overlapped, and glued in place, dot A will become one point of the star. Before using any glue, read through the next step and gently coax and curl each segment into a cone form.

4 To indicate the shaded glue area on each segment, draw a light pencil line from dot A1 to dot B1 on the right side of the paper, as shown on drawing 2. Spread glue on the shaded triangular area of one segment. Working quickly, roll the sides of the segment to create the star tip shown in drawing 3 by pulling point B1 down to the left to meet dot B1, and then overlapping it by pulling point C1 down to the right to meet dot C1. The overlapped lower edges should match precisely.

5 Repeat step 4 to form each star tip. Before adding glue to the final segment, form a loop of monofilament and tape it just below point A5 with the loop extending beyond the star.

MATERIALS

For one 3 7/8-inch (9.8-cm) diameter star

Pattern on page 110

5 1/2-inch (14.0-cm) square of acetate

5 1/2-inch (14.0-cm) square of stationery or origami paper

5-inch (12.7-cm) length of monofilament

NOTE: This design works well only with lightweight paper.

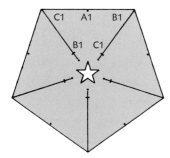

1. CUT SEGMENTS IN PENTAGON.

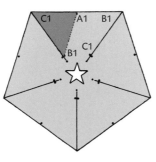

2. MARK GUIDELINE FOR GLUE AREA ON FIRST SEGMENT. SPREAD GLUE ON SHADED AREA.

3. CURL AND GLUE FIRST SEGMENT TO FORM ONE POINT OF STAR.

PUMPKIN CHAIN

Interlocking pumpkin faces link together to create a Halloween chain of jack-o'-lanterns. Enlarge or reduce the pattern, as you please, keeping in mind that the smaller the pattern, the lighter in weight the pumpkin paper should be so that it can be softly folded to interlock the links. Likewise, if the pattern is enlarged, the pumpkin paper must be heavy enough so that the jaw of the top pumpkin can support the chain of those below it. Directions for making a duplex paper variation of the chain are provided in the final step of the instructions for this project.

1   Photocopy or trace the pattern and glue it to acetate. Cut out the pumpkin and the facial features.

2   Score and fold each piece of paper in half crosswise to make a 3 1/4- by 3-inch (8.3- by 7.6-cm) format. Align the "place on fold" edge of the pattern along the folded edge of each paper. Holding the layers together with removable tape or paper clips, trace around the outside edge of the pumpkin and inside the facial features. Remove the pattern but leave the tape or clips in place.

3   Begin at the center of the unit, first cutting out the pumpkin face and then the exterior shape. Repeat to make fourteen links.

4   Link the first two pumpkins together. Referring to drawing 1, fold link 1, as shown. Completely unfold link 2 with the right side of the paper facing up. Gently curl or softly fold the upper single pumpkin portion of link 2, and insert it through the mouth of folded pumpkin link 1, from front to back. Referring to drawing 2, fold down pumpkin link 2 so that its stem hangs inside the tooth gap of pumpkin link 1. Continue to link the remaining pumpkins in the same way, one by one, from top to bottom.

MATERIALS

For one 30 1/2-inch (77.5-cm) chain

Pattern on page 108

3 1/4-inch (8.3-cm) square of acetate

Fourteen 3 1/4- by 6-inch (8.3- by 15.2-cm) pieces of paper, one for each 2 7/8- by 2 3/4-inch (7.3- by 7.0-cm) pumpkin link

NOTE: *The grain should run along the 6-inch (15.2-cm) length of the paper.*

5   To make the duplex paper variation, score and fold the paper in half crosswise, align the edges, and fasten the two paper layers together with removable tape. Align the stem edge of the pumpkin pattern on the folded edge of the paper and attach the pattern with removable tape. Draw within the features and around the edges of the pumpkin. Remove the pattern. Cut out the folded pumpkin, but do not cut out the face at this time. Unfold the pumpkin and cut out the face in only the pencil-marked single layer of paper. Join the pumpkins, linking only the face layers together. When the chain is complete, add a few dots of glue between the layers of each pumpkin, if necessary, to prevent curling of the paper.

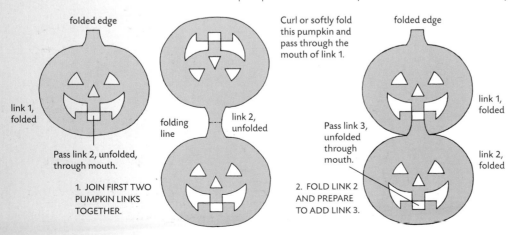

folded edge

link 1, folded

Pass link 2, unfolded, through mouth.

1. JOIN FIRST TWO PUMPKIN LINKS TOGETHER.

folding line

Curl or softly fold this pumpkin and pass through the mouth of link 1.

link 2, unfolded

2. FOLD LINK 2 AND PREPARE TO ADD LINK 3.

Pass link 3, unfolded through mouth.

folded edge

link 1, folded

link 2, folded

BAT WREATH

Although the lowly bat may not be at the top of everyone's list of favorite animals, bats certainly are hard-working, helpful little creatures. If bats were ever to do synchronized dancing in the night sky, this circle arrangement might be one of their routines.

1 Photocopy or trace the patterns and glue them to acetate. Pierce a few dots in the wreath pattern along every folding line. Cut out the eyes and both patterns.

2 Tape the wreath pattern to the right side of the paper and trace around it. Draw the eyes. Place pencil dots in the pattern holes to transfer only the folding lines indicated on drawing 1. Starting with the interior area, cut out the wreath and the eyes. Slide a large needle in and out of the eyes to make the edges even. Connect the pencil dots to draw the folding lines, but do not crease them.

3 Flip the wreath to the reverse side and hold the pattern against it. Transfer only the folding lines, including the ears, indicated on drawing 2, and connect the dots to draw them. Still working on the reverse side of the paper, score and crease the folding lines with mountain folds.

4 Flip the wreath over to the right side. Refer to drawing 1 and make mountain folds on all of the indicated lines.

5 Tape the base pattern to the paper, tracing around the edge and within the center. Place dots around the pattern inner and outer edges to transfer the dotted placement lines. Connect the dots to draw the placement lines and cut out the base.

6 Place the wreath, right side down, on a clean surface. The base will be glued to the wreath as on drawing 3. In order to align the bats well, the pencil-marked surface of the base should face up. Place glue along the folded side edges of the bat body (marked with an X on drawing 3). Noting the shaded area on drawing 3, also place glue in this position on the unmarked surface of the base. Place the base on the wreath, align the folding lines with the placement lines, and hold until dry. Repeat to glue each bat to the base.

7 Referring to drawing 4, use a toothpick to glue the bat wings to the unmarked surface of the base. Place glue along each wing folding line (marked with an X on drawing 4). Noting the shaded area on drawing 4, also place glue in this position on the unmarked surface of the base. Align the bat wing folding lines with the base placement lines, and hold until dry. Tie a loop of string between the bat wings.

MATERIALS

For one 5-inch (12.7-cm) diameter wreath

Patterns on page 111

6 3/4 inch (17.1-cm) square of acetate for wreath pattern

5 1/2-inch (14.0-cm) square of acetate for base pattern

6 3/4-inch (17.1-cm) square of sturdy paper for wreath

5 1/2-inch (14.0-cm) square of sturdy paper for base

5-inch (12.7-cm) length of string for hanging loop

1. SCORE THESE FOLDING LINES ON FRONT (RIGHT SIDE OF PAPER) OF EACH BAT.

2. SCORE THESE FOLDING LINES ON BACK (REVERSE SIDE OF PAPER) OF EACH BAT.

3. ON REVERSE SIDE OF WREATH, ALIGN FOLDED SIDE EDGES OF BAT BODY WITH PARALLEL PLACEMENT LINES ON LONG EDGES OF BASE AND GLUE IN PLACE.

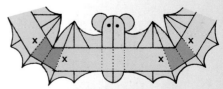

4. ON REVERSE SIDE OF WREATH, ALIGN FOLDED WINGS OF BAT WITH PLACEMENT LINES ON SHORT EDGES OF BASE AND GLUE IN PLACE.

GHOST BOX

Use a variety of papers to create ghost boxes for "Howl-o-ween" treats. Look for glitter-sparkled or glow-in-the-dark paper, or shimmery vellum. Cut out the facial features or color them in with felt tip pens. Fill up these little spirits with candy, a present, or a petite Halloween bouquet placed inside a tiny bottle.

1 Photocopy or trace the pattern. Cut out the pattern and the facial features to make a template.

2 Place the pattern on the paper and anchor it with removable tape or paper clips. Trace around the shape and within the features. Remove the pattern.

3 Cut out the ghost box and score all of the folding lines where they are indicated with broken lines on the pattern. Color or cut out the facial features. Fold the unit on all of the scored lines. Curl the heads back and the arms forward.

4 Apply glue to the tabs along both edges of the front of the ghost. Fold up the sides and press the ghost glue tabs inside of the side pieces. Repeat this step to glue the back of the ghost to the tabs.

MATERIALS

For one 2 3/4- by 3 1/4- by 1 1/4-inch (7.0- by 8.3- by 3.2-cm) box

Pattern on page 109

6 1/4- by 8 1/2-inch (15.9- by 21.6-cm) piece of paper

Fine-line felt tip pen for face, optional

WITCH HAT CORNUCOPIA

Stash a cache of Halloween tricks and treats inside this little hat or fill it with a tiny bunch of dried flowers. If you plan to make lots of hats for a party occasion, back the paper patterns with acetate to make them long-lasting and easy to handle.

1 Trace or photocopy the patterns and cut them out. Pierce the placement lines on the crown, brim, hatband, and optional liner.

2 Tape or clip the crown and brim patterns onto the paper. Trace around the edges of both patterns and within the "cut out" area of the brim. Before removing the crown pattern, use pencil dots to transfer the placement of the shaded glue tab and all of the segments around the curved edge of the crown. Before removing the brim pattern, transfer the straight glue tab line as well as the circular folding line around the base of the center glue tabs. Then add tiny pinholes around the center area of the brim pattern, placing one hole at the top and one hole at the base of each center glue tab cutting line.

3 Remove the patterns. Before cutting out the crown, score all of the segments marked on the pattern. Coax the piece into the form of a cone. Spread glue on the shaded tab and hold it until dry. Before cutting out the brim, cut, from pinhole to pinhole, all of the glue tabs around the center. Fold up the center glue tabs. Apply glue to the large shaded glue tab, overlap the opposite edge to form the brim, and hold until dry.

4 Spread a $1/4$-inch (0.6-cm) band of glue on the outside open edge of the conical crown (the hatband area). Hold the brim in one hand so the cupped side is facing up. Drop the pointed end of the crown into the center opening of the brim. Align the edges of the crown and brim. Flip the crown over so that the point is facing up. Press the brim glue tabs against the glue band around the outside of the crown. Cut one hatband and glue it on the crown to conceal the brim glue tabs.

5 Glue one end of the ribbon handle at each X mark inside the hat. If you are not adding a liner to the hat, use a paper punch to cut two small circles from the hat paper scraps and glue them over the ribbon ends inside the hat.

6 Use the pattern to draw and cut one optional liner piece. Spread glue inside the rim of the hat. Curl the liner paper into a small cone, right side inside, and push it inside the crown. Release the liner and fit it against the inside of the crown, aligning the edge of the liner with the edge of the brim. Glue the shaded overlapping edge.

MATERIALS

For one 3 $5/8$- by 4-inch (9.2- by 10.2-cm) hat

Patterns on page 112

4 $1/4$- by 9 $1/4$-inch (10.8- by 23.5-cm) piece of paper for crown

4-inch (10.2-cm) square of lightweight paper for hat liner, optional

1 $3/4$- by 5-inch (4.4- by 12.7-cm) piece of paper for hatband

7-inch (17.8-cm) length of black ribbon, $1/8$ inch (0.3 cm) wide

PUMPKIN PACKAGES

Pick your favorite package—a box or a basket, which should it be? To emphasize the jack-o'-lantern smile on either one, glue a translucent or opaque hexagon of contrasting paper inside the pumpkin behind the cut-out face.

MATERIALS

For one 2¼- by 2½-inch (5.7- by 6.4-cm) box

Patterns on page 113

6½-inch (16.5-cm) square of pumpkin-colored paper for box

2½-inch (6.4-cm) square of paper for face backing, optional

2-inch (5.1-cm) square of green paper for stem

BOX

1 Trace the pumpkin box and stem patterns with all of the markings or photocopy them. Glue the patterns to acetate if you wish. Use a large needle to pierce the pumpkin in a few places along the folding lines as well as each of the six dots on the box top. Cut out the facial features. Cut out the entire pattern.

2 Place the pumpkin box pattern on the right side of the orange paper and anchor it in place with removable tape or paper clips. Trace around the shape and within the features. Transfer all of the folding lines and the dots on the box top by placing a pencil point in the pierced pattern holes. Remove the pattern and cut out the face. Score the folding lines using a craft knife to connect the pencil dots you have made on the paper. Cut out the box. If desired, use the hexagon pattern to cut a contrasting piece of paper and glue it in place on the reverse side of the pumpkin face.

3 To assemble the box, place glue on the tabs bordering the sides of the box front. Fold up the side panels and press them to the glue tabs. Repeat this procedure on the back of the box.

4 Place the stem pattern on the right side of the green paper and draw around it. Make pencil dots along the top and bottom pattern edges to mark the placement of the vertical folding lines on the stem. Use a pin to completely pierce the paper layer at the five places where the single horizontal folding line intersects with the vertical folding lines on the pattern. Remove the stem pattern and use a craft knife to connect the pencil dots with lightly scored vertical lines on the right side of the paper.

Flip the paper over to the reverse side and connect the five pin holes with a craft knife, scoring a horizontal line completely across the lower notched end of the stem. Cut out the stem.

5 Flip the stem over to the right side of the paper and make a mountain fold on each scored vertical line. Apply glue to the right side of the side tab, form a tube, and overlap the glue tab with the opposite edge of the stem. Press the edges together. When the piece is dry, glue the stem to the pumpkin box, fanning the notches and aligning the point of each little triangle with one of the dots on the box top.

BASKET

1 To make the basket pattern, trace the pumpkin pattern, omitting the shaded box top and flaps. Also trace the basket handle pattern. If you are photocopying the pattern, you can cut off the shaded box top and flaps when you cut out the pattern. Glue the patterns to acetate if you wish. Use a large needle to pierce the pumpkin in a few places along the folding lines. Cut out the facial features to make a template. Punch out the holes on the basket sides and cut out the pattern.

2 Place the pumpkin basket pattern on the right side of the orange paper and anchor it in place with removable tape or paper clips. Trace around the shape and within the features and the punched out holes. Transfer all of the folding lines by placing a pencil point in the pierced pattern holes. Remove the pattern. Cut out the face. Punch out the holes on the sides. Score the folding lines using a craft knife to connect the pencil dots you have made on the paper. Cut out the box. If desired, use the hexagon pattern to cut a contrasting piece of paper and glue it in place on the reverse side of the pumpkin face.

3 To assemble the box, place glue on the tabs bordering the sides of the basket front. Fold up the side panels and press them to the glue tabs. Repeat the procedure on the back of the basket.

4 Place one end of the handle in one of the holes on the basket sides, passing the strip from the outside of the pumpkin to the inside. Apply a dot of glue on the end of the strip and press the end to the inside of the handle. Repeat this procedure with the opposite end of the handle.

MATERIALS

For one 2 1/4- by 3 5/8-inch (5.7- by 9.2-cm) basket

Patterns on page 113

6 1/2-inch (16.5-cm) square of pumpkin-colored paper for basket

2 1/2-inch (6.4-cm) square of paper for face backing, optional

1- by 6 1/4-inch (2.5- by 15.9-cm) piece of green paper for basket handle

Paper punch, 1/8-inch (0.3-cm) diameter

CHAIR PLACE CARDS

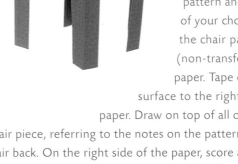

Let these personalized little chairs invite your guests to "please, be seated," at your Thanksgiving table. Write each name on the chair seat or back rest.

1 Photocopy the patterns and roughly trim around the chair pattern and the seat cover pattern of your choice. Tape or paper clip the chair pattern to the back (non-transfer side) of the transfer paper. Tape or clip the transfer surface to the right side of the chair paper. Draw on top of all of the lines.

2 Cut out the chair piece, referring to the notes on the pattern when cutting the area around the chair back. On the right side of the paper, score all of the broken lines except the two short X-marked lines at the base of the chair back. Flip the chair piece over to the reverse side and score the two short X-marked lines. Write a name on the chair at this time.

3 Flip the chair piece to the right side of the paper. Fold up the chair back, making valley folds on the two short X-marked lines. Make mountain folds on all of the remaining scored lines.

4 Rotate the chair 180 degrees so the reverse side of the back is facing toward you and the chair seat is facing away from you. Referring to drawing 1, fold down the A tab and spread it with glue. Still working on the reverse side and referring to drawing 2, swing down the back legs and overlap tab A with the B tabs. Hold until dry.

5 Again, rotate the chair 180 degrees so the seat faces toward you. Apply glue to the shaded glue tabs, place them behind the front legs, and hold until dry.

6 Select the seat cover pattern of your choice and transfer the pattern to the paper. Cut out the seat cover. Seat cover 1 is simply glued onto the chair seat. To attach seat cover 2, place the chair so the seat faces toward you. Spread glue on the reverse side of the entire seat cover and place it on the chair seat with the notched area at the back. Fold down both side edges and fold the A tabs against the front of the seat. Fold the B tab down over the A tabs. Rotate the chair so the reverse side of the chair back faces you. Fold down the C tab.

MATERIALS

For one 1¹/₂- by 1¹/₂- by 4¹/₄-inch (3.8- by 3.8- by 10.8-cm) chair

Patterns on page 114

6¹/₂-inch (16.5-cm) square of **sturdy paper for chair**

6¹/₂-inch (16.5-cm) square of **erasable transfer paper**

3-inch (7.6-cm) square of paper **for seat cover**

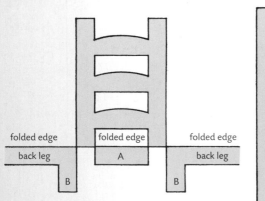

1. ON REVERSE SIDE OF CHAIR BACK, FOLD DOWN TAB A AND SPREAD WITH GLUE.

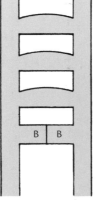

2. ON REVERSE SIDE OF CHAIR BACK, SWING DOWN BACK LEGS, OVERLAPPING TAB A WITH B TABS.

TWIN HOUSE CARDS

This is a bonus project, because you can almost make two cards at once, and you don't need to do any drawing at all. Make the first card by cutting right through a photocopied pattern, reserving all of the cut-out colored pieces of paper, as well as the stencil-like pattern framework. Then tape the pattern framework onto another folded piece of paper and, using the pattern as a template, simply fit in the cutouts like puzzle pieces and glue them in place to make a second card.

1 Photocopy the pattern and cut around the outline of the square. To make the first card, score and fold the indigo paper in half crosswise. Unfold the card and tape it to your work surface. Align the top edge of the pattern with the folded edge of the card. Tape the pattern securely in place and draw around the outside edge.

2 Cut out all stars, stripes, windows, and the house. Reserve every cut-out piece of indigo paper, placing the pieces in precise order on a nearby piece of paper. Do not rotate the pieces or flip them over to the reverse side. To make the second card, reserve the pattern framework and the pattern pieces for the house front and side.

3 Remove the indigo paper from the work surface. Fold it and hold the edges together with paper clips or tape. Cut out the square and unfold it so the inside of the card faces you. Place a piece of scrap paper on the work surface and top it with the unfolded card. Carefully spread a thin layer of glue on only the cut area (the reverse side of the card front). Align one cut edge of the brick paper with the folding line on the glued side of the indigo card. Press firmly. Flip the card over to the right side and allow it to dry. If necessary, trim the edges to align.

4 To determine the correct window placement, temporarily place the reserved pattern pieces for the house front and side on the card front, aligning the cut edges of the patterns with the cut-out areas on the card. Glue the reserved indigo windows within the window openings of the house front and side patterns. Remove the patterns.

5 To make the second card, score and fold the stone paper in half and tape it to your work surface. Align the top edge of the reserved pattern framework along the folded edge of the paper. Tape the pattern securely in place and draw around the outside edge. Leaving the pattern framework in place as a "mask" and working quickly on one small area at a time, spread glue within the open areas of the card. Immediately fit in the proper indigo shapes and press firmly. When the glue is dry, remove the pattern. Hold the card layers together with clips and cut out the card on the outline.

MATERIALS

For two cards, each 4¹/₄-inch (10.8-cm) square

Pattern on page 113

4¹/₂- by 9-inch (11.4- by 22.9-cm) piece of sturdy indigo paper

4¹/₂-inch (11.4-cm) square of brick paper

4¹/₂- by 9-inch (11.4- by 22.9-cm) piece of sturdy stone paper

Two envelopes, 4³/₈ by 5³/₄ inches (11.1 by 14.6 cm), or Envelope B pattern, page 88, and instructions, pages 86 to 87

CHAPTER FIVE

WINTER TIMES

❄

Toss another log on the fire and sprinkle a few more marshmallows in the cocoa, winter times are here! Make a little paper magic using traditional symbols of faith, love, peace, and joy to brighten the days and warm the nights of this dark and frosty season. To deck your halls or convey your good wishes, angels and snowflakes, cookies and presents await your creative hands.

COOKIE *SHEET* BOOK

Open the cookie sheet cover of this shiny little book and you will find recipes for a baker's dozen of tasty treats. Decorative paper punches will help you to whip up a big batch of your favorites in no time at all.

❄

1 Photocopy or trace the patterns and the pattern guide. Cut out the patterns and punch out the holes.

2 On each index card lightly draw a $3/4$-inch (1.9-cm) margin along the left front edge. On the same edge of each card, draw and score a $1/2$-inch (1.3-cm) margin. Fold each card back and forth on the scored line so the card pages will turn easily when the book is bound. On the reverse side of each card lightly draw a $3/4$-inch (1.9-cm) margin on the left edge. Flip the cards over to the right side. Use the pattern guide as a template to draw and punch out the holes on the left edge of the cards. Write the recipes within the margins and put the cards aside.

3 Tape or clip the cover pattern to the foil board. Draw around the shapes and mark the holes and score lines. Cut out the covers. Lightly score the folding lines on each side of each cover and crease them. Punch out the holes.

4 Referring to drawing 1, place the front and back covers side by side, metallic side down. Spread glue on the shaded area of the back cover as shown. Referring to drawing 2 and aligning the holes, overlap the glue tab of the back with the front cover. Allow to dry.

5 Stack the recipe cards and open the book cover. Place the stack on the back cover, aligning the holes. Wrap the cover around the edge of the stack and close it, aligning the holes. Wrap the ribbon ends in transparent tape to make them look like shoelaces. Working on the book front, pass one end of the ribbon from front to back through the topmost hole and the other end from front to back through the lowest hole. Align the ribbon ends and pull them tightly to the back of the book. Bring both ends back to the front through the center hole, pull tightly, tie a bow, and trim the ends.

6 Spread glue on the scraps of frosting-colored paper and sprinkle them with glitter before the glue dries. Punch out six frosting shapes and glue each one to a scrap of cookie-colored paper, leaving at least $1/4$ inch (0.6 cm) between the shapes. Cut out the cookies leaving a narrow margin, less than $1/8$ inch (0.3 cm), beyond the frosting edge. Draw a thin brown edge around each of the cookies and glue them on the front cover.

MATERIALS

For one 3 1/2- by 5 1/4-inch (8.9- by 13.3-cm) book

Patterns on page 115

Paper punch, $1/8$-inch (0.3-cm) diameter

Thirteen 3- by 5-inch (7.6- by 12.7-cm) index cards

Two $3 3/4$- by $6 1/2$-inch (9.5- by 16.5-cm) pieces of lightweight foil board

Scraps of frosting-colored and cookie-colored paper

Glitter

Decorative paper punches with 1-inch (2.5-cm) motifs

Felt tip pen a little darker than cookie paper

14-inch (35.6-cm) length of ribbon

Envelope, $4 1/8$ by $5 1/2$ inches (10.5 by 14.0 cm), or Envelope A pattern, page 87, and instructions, pages 86 to 87

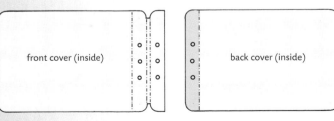

1. SPREAD GLUE ON BACK COVER HINGE.

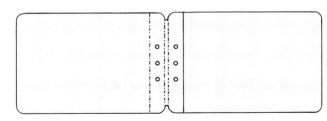

2. OVERLAP BACK COVER WITH FRONT COVER.

COCOA CARD

Topped with cream or dotted with little marshmallows, a cup of cocoa is the picture of comfort all winter long. You can warm someone's heart with this cozy card, filled to the brim with your good wishes.

❄

1 Photocopy or trace the patterns and cut them out. Use a pin to pierce the placement line for the cocoa on the mug.

2 Score the mug paper in half crosswise and fold the card. Align the "place on fold" edge of the mug pattern with the folded edge of the card, holding it in place with paper clips or removable tape. Transfer the cocoa placement line onto the mug. Draw around the shape. Remove the pattern.

3 Anchor the folded card layers together with tape or clips. Use a craft knife on a protected work surface to cut out the mug. Place the cocoa pattern on your selected paper, draw around the edge, and remove the pattern. Cut out the cocoa and glue it in place on the mug.

4 Place the pocket overlay pattern on your selected paper, draw around the pattern edge, remove the pattern, and cut out the pocket. Flip the pocket over to the reverse side. Referring to the pattern for placement, spread glue around the shaded edges and place the pocket overlay on the mug, overlapping the cocoa. Allow to dry. Be sure that the mug and pocket layers are glued together well along the side edges, especially near the pocket top. If necessary, trim the edges of the layers to align.

5 Tape or clip the spoon pattern to the paper. Draw around the spoon, remove the pattern, and cut out the shape. To add the cocoa to the spoon, trace the oval pattern at the center of the spoon and cut it out. Place the pattern on the cocoa paper, draw around the shape, and cut it out. Glue the shape to the spoon. To make the candy stick, score and fold the striped paper in half lengthwise, right side outside, and glue the inside surfaces together. Insert the spoon or candy stick in the mug pocket.

MATERIALS

For one 4- by 4⁹/₁₆-inch (10.2- by 11.6-cm) card

Patterns on page 116

4¹/₂- by 9¹/₂-inch (11.4- by 24.1-cm) piece of sturdy paper for mug

4¹/₂-inch (11.4-cm) square of paper for pocket overlay

3¹/₂-inch (8.9-cm) square of paper for cocoa

2- by 6¹/₂-inch (5.1- by 16.5-cm) piece of sturdy paper for spoon, or 1- by 5-inch (2.5- by 12.7-cm) piece of paper cut diagonally from striped paper for candy stick

Envelope, 4¹/₄ by 5¹/₈ inches (10.8 by 13.0 cm), or Envelope C pattern, page 88, and instructions, pages 86 to 87

COUNTRY CHURCH BOX

Inspired by a vintage Christmas decoration, this little church is the perfect size to hold a small gift, rest on a tabletop, or be tucked into the branches of a Christmas tree. The church could also be a meaningful Easter decoration or a charming way to present a wedding gift certificate. Church-building is a project best suited to somewhat experienced paper crafters. For a time-saving variation, cut the window frames and door on church section A only and don't add the translucent paper windows. Instead, use duplex paper for the church so that the color inside will show in the open windows.

❋

1 Photocopy both pattern pages, or trace the pattern pieces and rough-cut around them, leaving a narrow margin around each piece. Because of the small cut-out details it is best to cut right through the pattern and paper to make the pieces for this project.

2 On the right side of the church paper, use removable tape to attach the patterns for section A and section B. Tape the paper to your cutting mat.

3 Cutting right through the patterns and the paper, first cut the interior details such as the window frames and the door cutting line. If not adding translucent windows to the church, do not cut out the windows on section B. Use a pin to lightly transfer the ends of all the folding lines.

4 Cut on the outlines of sections A and B, reserving the leftover paper. Remove the patterns and use a craft knife to score the folding lines (except the door) on the right side (outside) of both pieces. Flip over section A and score the door folding lines on the reverse side (inside). Crease both of the pieces on the folding lines and set them aside.

5 If adding windows, cut the window patterns on the outlines. Fold the translucent paper in half. Trace around the small window pattern once. Trace around the large window pattern four times. Cut out the windows. On the reverse side of sections A and B, glue the windows in place. There will be one large window left over.

6 Apply glue to the tabs on sections A and B and assemble the church. Use lots of removable tape to hold the church together until the glue dries. Remove the tape.

7 On a reserved piece of church paper, tape the steeple pattern and paper to the cutting mat. Cut out the opening in the steeple and use a pin to lightly transfer the ends of the folding lines. Cut out the piece and score all of the folding lines on the right side (outside) of the steeple. Fold all of the scored lines and set the piece aside.

8 Cut the remaining church paper into two same-size pieces, tape the pieces together, add the roof support pattern, and tape the combined unit to your cutting mat. Cut out the window opening on the roof support pattern and use

MATERIALS

For one 2⁷/₈- by 5- by 7⁷/₈-inch
(7.3- by 12.7- by 20.0-cm) church

Patterns on pages 118 and 119

11-inch (27.9-cm) square of sturdy paper for church, steeple, and roof supports

6- by 9-inch (15.2- by 22.9-cm) piece of paper for church roof and steeple roof

6-inch (15.2-cm) square of glassine paper or sheer vellum for windows, optional

Glitter, optional

a pin to lightly transfer the ends of the folding lines. Cut out the roof supports, score the folding lines on the right side (outside) of the pieces, and then crease them on the folding lines.

9   Cut a 6-inch (15.2-cm) square of the roof paper. Score and fold it to make a 3- by 6-inch (7.6- by 15.2-cm) piece and set it aside, reserving all of the scraps. On the roof pattern piece, cut precisely along the edge marked "place on fold of roof paper." Align the trimmed edge of the roof pattern on the folded edge of the roof paper, taping the pattern in place. Cut out the slots on the roof. Cut out the roof and remove the pattern. Unfold the roof so the reverse side (inside) faces you. Hold the roof pattern against each side of the fold and use a pin to lightly transfer the placement of the glue areas. Connect the pin holes with pencil lines to draw the placement of the glue areas. Apply glue to the tabs on the roof support pieces and place the church roof on top of them.

10 Use the remaining scrap of roof paper to make the steeple roof, using a pin to transfer the folding lines. Cut out the steeple roof and remove the pattern. Fold the steeple roof on the scored lines. Apply glue to the tab, assemble the roof, and allow it to dry.

11 Place glue on the tabs at the top of the steeple. Set the steeple roof in place. Rotate the steeple to check the accuracy of the roof placement so it will not be askew. If desired, spread a layer of glue on the steeple roof and the church roof, sprinkle them with glitter, and allow them to dry.

12 Apply glue to the reverse side (inside) of the tabs at the bottom of the steeple. Insert the tabs in the church roof, fold up the tabs, and allow the piece to dry. Set the roof unit on the church, placing the roof props inside the church walls.

FRINGED PINE TREE

On one of the many occasions that my mother created Christmas magic for me, she produced a snowy winter scene right in the middle of our dining room table. Instead of smoke and mirrors she used soap and mirrors to make a pond (the mirror) banked with drifts of dry soap powder snow. There were lots of little trees planted in the powder and a herd of white celluloid reindeer, speckled with tarnished glitter. Use this tree design to create your own winter wonderland, and if you're looking for a paper-cutting challenge, reduce the pattern by half and make miniature trees, pictured on page 68.

❄

1 Photocopy or trace the patterns, but do not cut them out.

2 Stack the papers, aligning and taping them together in this order, from the bottom of the stack: green paper, right side up; transfer paper, transfer surface down; patterns, right side up.

3 Using a pencil and a straightedge, firmly draw on all of the pattern lines. Remove the patterns and the transfer paper, reserving it for another use.

4 Cut the straight fringe lines on each tier of the tree with a craft knife. Then cut out the entire piece, using scissors around the curved edges to avoid damaging the fringes. On tier 1, pierce through the trunk placement line with a pin so it will be visible inside the completed tree.

5 Curl tier 1 to help it take the proper form. Spread glue on the tab and overlap it with the opposite straight edge of the tier, holding it until dry. Cut and glue tier 2 in the same way. Align tier 2 on the proper placement line of tier 1 and glue it in place. Also complete tier 3 and glue it in place on tier 1. Form a cone with tier 4 and glue it on top of the tree.

6 To make the trunk, roll the brown piece of paper lengthwise to form a $4^{1}/_{8}$-inch (10.5-cm) cylinder. Overlap the edges $^{1}/_{4}$ inch (0.6 cm) and glue them together. When dry, add glue to the edge of one end of the cylinder. Turn the tree upside down and attach the trunk to its placement line inside the tree on tier 1.

7 To make a 3-inch (7.6-cm) tree, photocopy the pattern at 50 percent. Use a $4^{1}/_{4}$- by $5^{1}/_{2}$-inch (10.8- by 14.0-cm) piece of stationery-weight paper for the tree and complete steps 1 through 5, above. To make the trunk, refer to step 6, above, substituting a $1^{5}/_{8}$- by $2^{1}/_{8}$-inch (4.1- by 5.4-cm) piece of brown paper. Roll and glue the paper to form a $2^{1}/_{8}$-inch (5.4-cm) cylinder with the edges overlapped $^{1}/_{4}$ inch (0.6 cm). Complete step 6, above.

MATERIALS

For one $5^{3}/_{8}$-inch (13.6-cm) tree

Patterns on page 117

$8^{1}/_{2}$- by 11-inch (21.6- by 27.9-cm) piece of erasable transfer paper

$8^{1}/_{2}$- by 11-inch (21.6- by 27.9-cm) piece of sturdy green paper for tree

3- by $4^{1}/_{8}$-inch (7.6- by 10.5-cm) piece of brown paper for trunk

Large needle or pin

CHOIR ANGEL

Whether standing for a solo, or in a duet, trio, or full choir, this little angel will welcome the holidays on a joyful note.

❄

1 Photocopy or trace the patterns with all the markings and cut them out.

2 Use removable tape or paper clips to anchor the patterns on the paper. Trace around the shapes and transfer all of the markings. Remove the patterns and cut out the pieces. On the halo/sleeve unit, cut around the halo, cut the slots indicated, and score the folding lines. Also make 1/8-inch (0.3-cm) vertical cuts on the base of the halo. On the head/robe/wing unit, cut around the head, cut the slots indicated, and score the folding lines. If a decorative edge is desired, cut it outside the pattern outline. Use decorative edge scissors to cut around the outside edge of the head/robe/wing unit and around the outside edge of the collar and the halo/sleeve unit. Do not attempt to cut the head, halo, or slots with decorative scissors.

3 Hold the head/robe/wing unit with the robe color facing you (the wing color will be on the reverse side). Make a valley (V) fold along each wing. With one wing in each hand, form the cone shaped robe by switching the wings to your opposite hands as you interlock the slots at the center back. Do not glue.

4 Hold the halo/sleeve unit with the halo color facing you (the sleeve color will be on the reverse). Make mountain (M) and valley (V) folds as indicated on the pattern. Flatten the unit and spread glue on the shaded area above the halo. Referring to the drawing at right, softly fold point X and point Y above the halo down to meet point X and point Y below the halo, covering the shaded area and aligning the center back and lower edges. Allow to dry.

5 On the head/robe/wing unit, pull the wings together at the center back of the angel, moving them away from the robe. Referring to the pattern, spread glue on the shaded area of the robe. Slide the halo/sleeve unit down onto the angel, engaging the slots at the center back. Hold until dry.

6 Score the folding lines on the collar and cut two short slots where indicated. Make valley folds on the collar score lines and wrap the collar around the neck, engaging the halo in the slots. Spread glue on the underside of the shaded area of the collar. Align the straight collar edges with the center back of the angel, under the wings. The top straight edges of the collar glue tabs should align with the folding line at the base of the halo.

7 Spread glue under each wing tab at the center back from the top of the neck to the bottom of the robe. Press the tab against the back of the angel and hold until dry.

MATERIALS

For one 3 1/2-inch (8.9-cm) angel

Patterns on page 122

Scalloped-edge scissors, optional

6- by 8-inch (15.2- by 20.3-cm) piece of lightweight foil paper or duplex paper

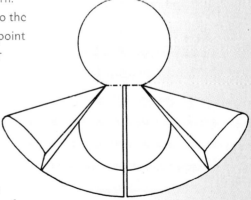

SOFTLY FOLD AND GLUE
UNIT TO FORM SLEEVES.

STAR OF DAVID

Interlock two slotted strips of paper to create a chunky Star of David ornament, and add a bottom to make the star into a basket. Accuracy is essential for an exact fit of the two star sections, so it is best to photocopy the pattern instead of tracing it.

❄

1 Photocopy the patterns, glue them to acetate, and cut them out. Pierce the folding lines on each pattern in several places and pierce the hanging loop position on the glue tab.

2 Tape or clip the strip pattern on the paper. Trace around the pattern and within each slot. Transfer the folding lines by placing a sharp pencil in the pattern pinholes. Repeat to make another strip. Cut out both strips, cutting the slots like narrow channels. Check the front and back of each strip and, if necessary, trim the edges of the slots so they are perfectly straight and neat. Score the folding lines.

3 Crease one strip to form a triangle. Tape the cut ends of the looped thread to the glue tab. Apply glue to the tab, covering the taped ends of the thread. Press the strip ends together to form a triangle. Use removable tape to temporarily hold the strip ends together if necessary. Allow to dry.

4 Crease and glue the remaining strip to form a triangle. Referring to drawing 1, place the triangle with the hanging loop on your work surface with the slots facing up. Place the other triangle as shown with the slots facing down. Referring to drawing 2, lift the lower triangle and place it directly on top of the triangle remaining on your work surface. Align the slotted edges of both triangles and gently engage the slots to form a star.

5 To make the basket, complete steps 1 through 4, reserving a 2 1/2- by 3-inch (6.4- by 7.6-cm) piece of paper and omitting the hanging loop. Tape or clip the base pattern onto the reserved paper scrap, trace around the pattern, and transfer the folding lines. Cut out the base and score and crease the folding lines. Apply glue to the tabs and insert them up inside the center bottom section of the star.

MATERIALS

For one 3 1/2-inch (8.9-cm) ornament or basket

Patterns on page 123

3- by 12-inch (7.6- by 30.5-cm) strip of acetate

3- by 12-inch (7.6- by 30.5-cm) piece of sturdy paper or lightweight card stock

5 1/2-inch (14.0-cm) length of metallic thread or monofilament

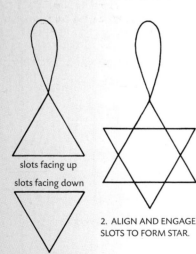

slots facing up

slots facing down

1. PLACE TRIANGLES ON WORK SURFACE.

2. ALIGN AND ENGAGE SLOTS TO FORM STAR.

SPINNING DREIDEL CARD

For Hanukkah make a spinning dreidel card with paste-on or cut-out Star of David motifs at the center. The dreidel folds flat to fit inside an envelope easily and it twirls playfully when opened and hung for display.

❄

1 Trace or photocopy the patterns and cut them out. Also cut out the star at the center of each pattern piece.

2 Fold the dreidel pattern in half lengthwise. Score and fold each piece of dreidel paper in half lengthwise and tape or clip the folded pattern on one folded paper. Draw around the shape. Leaving the tape or clips in place, cut out the dreidel, remove the pattern, and unfold the dreidel. Tape or clip the unfolded pattern on the unfolded dreidel and draw within the star at the center. Draw and cut the remaining three dreidels, marking the star on each one.

3 If making the card with the cut-out star center, cut that penciled area now and skip to step 4. To make the card with the foil stars at the center, draw around the outer edge of the star hanger pattern and cut out four stars. On the reverse side of the foil, score and fold each star through the center and glue one in place within the penciled outline on each dreidel. Cover each dreidel with scrap paper and flatten the unit with the edge of a ruler to join the two papers completely. Fold and unfold each dreidel a few times to help the star find its place, so the foil will not wrinkle or lift when the card is folded and unfolded.

4 Tape one cut end of the thread at the X on the reverse side of one dreidel and set it aside. Determine the color sequence of the dreidels, select one, fold it in half, and spread one half section with glue. Place the next folded dreidel on top and press the pieces together with the edges aligned. Glue the remaining folded dreidels together to make a stack that resembles a closed book. With this book image in mind, add glue to the front and back "covers" and fully open the book, bringing the front and back covers together just as you would never do with a real book! Press these two surfaces together with their edges aligned. Check the top and bottom of the dreidel to see if the union of the four sections looks good at the center and make adjustments if necessary. When dry, trim the edges to match.

5 Stack and tape or clip the star hanger papers together with the pattern on top of the stack. Draw around and within the star hanger shape. Remove the pattern, but keep the papers joined together. First cut out the center star and then the outside edges. Tape one end of the thread at the X on the reverse side of one star hanger, spread glue on the reverse side of the remaining one, and press the two stars together with their edges aligned. If necessary, trim the edges to match when dry.

MATERIALS

For one 3 1/8- by 4 3/4-inch (7.9- by 12.1-cm) card

Patterns on page 123

Four 3 1/2- by 5-inch (8.9- by 12.7-cm) pieces of sturdy paper, each a different color, for dreidel

Four 2 1/2-inch (6.4-cm) squares of foil for center star, optional

Two 2 1/2-inch (6.4-cm) squares of paper for star hanger

4 1/2-inch (11.4-cm) length of metallic thread or monofilament

Envelope, 3 7/8 by 5 3/8 inches (9.8 by 13.6 cm), or Envelope E pattern, page 89, and instructions, pages 86 to 87

PETITE PRESENTS

These little parcels are just the right size for packaging small, lightweight, unbreakable presents. Place a gift certificate inside the gift box and pop it into a shopping bag. Good things really do come in small packages!

❄

MINI SHOPPING BAG

1. Photocopy or trace the pattern and cut it out. Cut the handle slots on the bag top and the flaps on the bottom on the solid lines.

2. Tape or clip the papers together on your work surface in this order: gift wrap, right side up; transfer paper, right side down; pattern, right side up. Referring to drawing 1, draw on and around the pattern, transferring all of the cutting lines but only those folding lines indicated on the drawing. Score all of the folding lines shown on drawing 1. Cut out the bag, the handle slots, and the bottom flaps. Fold the scored lines, creasing them sharply, then unfold.

3. Flip the bag and pattern over to the reverse side. Place the transfer paper and pattern on the bag and transfer only the details shown on drawing 2. Remove the pattern and score all the folding lines. Fold the newly scored lines, creasing them sharply. Unfold. Turn to the right side (outside) of the bag.

4. Referring to drawing 3, mark, score, and fold two handles. Insert each handle in the slots on the right side (outside) of the bag top as shown in drawing 4. Align the handle tops with the bag top.

5. Flip the bag over to the reverse side. Place glue under the handle ends. Referring to drawing 5, align the handles in the glue areas and allow to dry. Fold the bag top over the handle ends and glue it in place as in drawing 6.

6. Diagonally fold the wide flaps on the bag bottom as in drawing 7. Unfold the flaps, apply glue, refold, and allow to dry. Fold the right edge glue tab towards the bag. Place glue on the tab surface facing up (the right side of the paper).

MATERIALS

For one 3- by 4¹/₂- by 1¹/₂-inch (7.6- by 11.4- by 3.8-cm) shopping bag

Pattern on page 120

7- by 10-inch (17.8- by 25.4-cm) piece of gift wrap paper for bag

Two ¹/₄- by 4¹/₈-inch (0.6- by 10.5-cm) strips of paper for handles.

7- by 10-inch (17.8- by 25.4-cm) piece of transfer paper

NOTE: *If bag paper is very thin, glue two layers together to make handles stronger.*

1. TRANSFER ALL CUTTING LINES AND ONLY THESE FOLDING LINES.

2. TRANSFER THESE DETAILS.

3. MARK, SCORE, AND FOLD HANDLES.

4. INSERT HANDLES IN SLOTS.

5. GLUE HANDLE ENDS.

6. FOLD DOWN AND GLUE TOP EDGE OF BAG, OVERLAPPING HANDLE ENDS.

7. FOLD BOTTOM FLAPS DIAGONALLY AND GLUE. FOLD SIDE GLUE TAB.

8. FOLD LEFT CUT EDGE OVER TO MEET RIGHT FOLDED EDGE OF BAG WHILE TUCKING SIDE FOLDS INSIDE BAG. PULL FOLDED BOTTOM FLAPS UP AND OUT TO SIDES.

9. LIFT UP TOP-POINTED FLAP, UNFOLDING BOTTOM FLAPS.

10. FOLD IN SIDE FLAPS AND TAPE TOGETHER AT CENTER.

11. FOLD, GLUE, AND OVERLAP BOTTOM FLAPS.

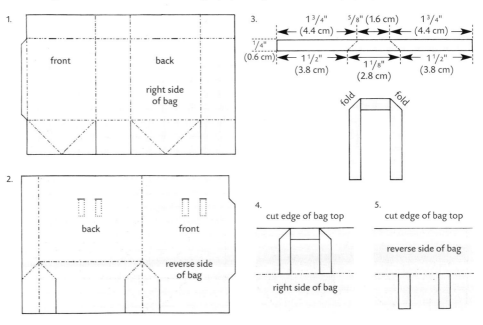

7 Referring to drawing 8, fold the left cut edge over to align with the right folded edge of the glue tab while tucking in the bag sides. Pull the bottom flaps up and out to each side as shown in drawing 8.

8 To create the bottom of the bag, lift up the top-pointed flap so the bag resembles drawing 9. Fold the side flaps in to meet at the center as in drawing 10. Tape the side flaps together at the center bottom. Referring to drawing 11, apply glue to the upper pointed flap and fold it down. Apply glue to the remaining pointed flap and fold it up to overlap the other flap.

TINY GIFT BOX

1 Trace or preferably photocopy the pattern. Cut out the pattern as well as the solid cutting lines and the slot. Score and crease the folding lines with mountain folds, then unfold. See steps 3 through 5, below, and practice folding the pattern to understand the box assembly.

2 Tape or clip the papers together on your work surface in this order: box paper, right side up; transfer paper, right side down; pattern, right side up. Draw on and around the pattern, transferring all of the details. Remove the pattern and the transfer paper, leaving the box-paper on your work surface. Make cuts on the solid lines. Score and crease the folding lines, making mountain folds. Unfold the box completely and flip it over to the reverse side (inside).

3 On one side of the box, fold both A panels toward each other so the edges with dots align. Butt the edges together without overlapping them, and tape them to each other. Repeat on the opposite side of the box.

4 On one side of the box, lift panel B up and over the joined A panels. Push panel C down inside the box and glue it in place. Repeat on the opposite side of the box.

5 Close the cover pushing both D panels inside the box front. Curl panel E slightly toward the box and gently push the lower portion into the slot.

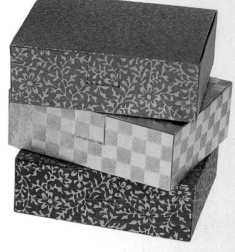

MATERIALS

For one 3- by 2 1/4- by 1-inch (7.6- by 5.7- by 2.5-cm) box

Pattern on page 121

8- by 8 1/2-inch (20.3- by 21.6-cm) piece of paper for box

7- by 10-inch (17.8- by 25.4-cm) piece of transfer paper

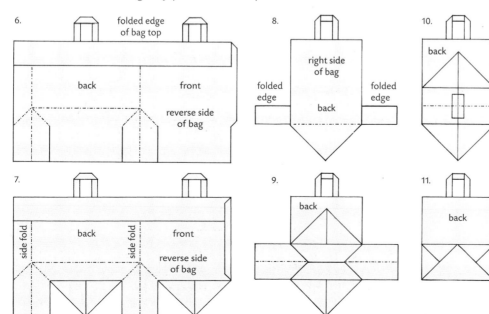

SNOWBABY PROJECTS

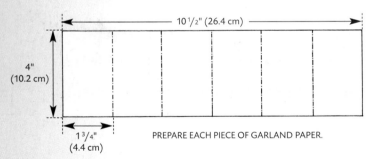

Little people and big hearts are the symbols for this group of cutouts. Hearts and hands together create a folded garland or a wreath.

❄

WREATH

1 Fold a 10 1/2-inch (26.4-cm) square of tracing paper into quarter sections. Align the straight edges of the wreath pattern section with the folds of the paper and trace the section four times to make a complete wreath pattern. Glue the complete pattern to acetate, if you wish, and cut it out. Pierce each folding line in a few places.

2 Tape or clip the pattern to the wreath paper and draw around it. Transfer the folding lines with pencil dots placed in the pinholes.

3 Starting at the center, cut out the wreath. Cut out and discard all of the X-marked negative areas. Score and fold the center line on every baby and heart. Flip the wreath over to the reverse side and score and fold each line between every heart and hand.

MATERIALS

For one 9 1/4-inch (23.5-cm) diameter wreath or 21-inch (53.3-cm) garland

Patterns on page 127

10 1/2-inch (26.7-cm) square of sturdy paper for wreath or two 4- by 10 1/2-inch (10.2- by 26.4-cm) pieces of stationery-weight paper for garland

GARLAND

1 Photocopy the garland pattern or trace it. Glue the pattern to acetate, if you wish, and cut it out. Pierce the folding lines in several places.

2 Referring to the drawing below, score and accordion-fold one piece of garland paper, creasing it sharply. Unfold the paper and tape or clip the pattern in place on one section, aligning the side edges. Draw around the pattern, remove it, and refold the paper, taping or clipping the edges together.

3 Starting with the area between the legs, cut out the shape. Unfold the garland and score and fold the center line on each baby and heart.

4 Repeat to make a second garland section. Tape the two sections together on the reverse side.

```
|←————————— 10 1/2" (26.4 cm) —————————→|

4"
(10.2 cm)

|← 1 3/4" →|
  (4.4 cm)    PREPARE EACH PIECE OF GARLAND PAPER.
```

PASTEL SNOWFLAKES

These somewhat challenging snowflakes will provide lots of practice in making mountain and valley folds. Instead of reaching for only your white and silver papers, consider using the soft colors of the winter sky, the way it looks just before the snow.

1 Trace or preferably photocopy the pattern, transferring all the markings. Do not cut out the pattern, but trim it to a 5-inch (12.7-cm) square.

2 Align and tape the papers together in this order, from the bottom of the stack: snowflake paper, right side up; transfer paper, transfer surface down; pattern, right side up.

3 Use a pencil and straightedge to draw all of the pattern lines. Remove the pattern and the transfer paper and save it for another use.

4 Score all of the folding lines that pass across the center, from edge to edge of the snowflake, and all of the short folding lines on each branch. Referring to drawing 1, use a pin to make a barely visible hole at each point where the folding lines intersect. Starting with the kite shapes around the center, cut out the snowflake.

5 Make mountain folds, creasing all of the folding lines that pass across the center of the snowflake. Place the work on a flat surface, align the cut edges as closely as possible, and crease sharply every time a fold is made. Flip the unfolded snowflake to the reverse side. Without additional scoring, make mountain folds on all the previously folded lines.

6 Referring to drawing 2, note the position of the X, and fold the snowflake in half, right side inside. Each branch, completed one at a time, will be a series of accordion folds. Refer to drawing 3 and make the first fold by holding the snowflake, somewhat unfolded, in both hands. Press the tip of your thumbnail against the first pinhole (marked by an X on drawing 2) and fold the branch down as in drawing 3. Unfold the branch somewhat. Pressing your thumbnail against the next pinhole, fold up the branch as in drawing 4. Unfold the branch somewhat. Press your thumb against the next pinhole and fold down the branch as in drawing 5. Repeat this entire step to fold each branch.

7 Fold the entire snowflake, referring to the pattern for placement of the mountain (M) and valley (V) folds. Pass one end of the monofilament through an existing pinhole at the top of a branch and knot the ends.

MATERIALS

For one 2 1/2-inch (6.4-cm) snowflake

Pattern on page 127

5-inch (12.7-cm) square of erasable transfer paper

5-inch (12.7-cm) square of stationery-weight paper

6-inch length of monofilament

NOTE: Stationery paper must be of a good quality to withstand folding it in two directions.

1. MAKE TINY PINHOLES AT INTERSECTING LINES ON EVERY BRANCH OF SNOWFLAKE.

2. FOLD SNOWFLAKE IN HALF THROUGH BRANCHES, RIGHT SIDE OUT.

3. FOLD BRANCH DOWN.

4. FOLD BRANCH UP.

5. FOLD BRANCH DOWN.

SANTA CORNUCOPIA

Here's your chance to stuff Santa with his favorite Christmas treats! When you select the materials to make him, be sure to choose an opaque white paper that is thin enough to form into a cone without folding and wrinkling it during the process.

❄

1 Photocopy or trace the patterns with all the markings and cut them out. Pierce a few dots along the glue tab and hat lines and around the face. On the face pattern make a template for the placement of the features by using paper punches to remove the eye, nose, and cheek circles. This is best done by placing an extra layer of paper behind the face pattern to add heft and create a sturdier cutting surface for the punches. Also pierce each end of the mouth and the slot for the moustache.

2 Use removable tape or paper clips to anchor the cornucopia pattern on the white paper and draw around the shape, transferring the placement lines with pencil dots. Also draw one support piece and two moustache pieces. On the light pink paper draw one face, lightly marking the features and the moustache slot. On the red paper draw two hats.

3 Cut out all the pieces. Use a ¹/₈-inch (0.3-cm) paper punch to make two black eyes and a ¹/₄-inch (0.6-cm) punch to make one red nose and two pink cheeks.

4 Glue the face to the cornucopia and cut the moustache slot. Insert both moustache tabs into the slot. Fold the tabs against the reverse side of the cornucopia and glue or tape them in place. Do not glue the moustache pieces on the face front. Glue the cheeks under the moustache and the red nose on top of it. Add black eyes and draw a red mouth. Glue the hat pieces in place.

5 Gently roll the cornucopia into a cone form. To do this, coax and curl the paper by pulling it over a straightedge. Place glue on the tab, form a cone, and hold the unit in place until dry. The tip of the cone might be troublesome, so use the point of a pencil with a broken lead as a helper in this area.

6 To make the cornucopia handles, interlock the circles at the hat top and glue them together. Glue the support piece below the interlocked area.

MATERIALS

For one 7-inch (17.8-cm) cornucopia

Patterns on page 125

8-inch (20.3-cm) square of lightweight white paper

2-inch (5.1-cm) square of lightweight pale pink paper

1-inch (2.5-cm) squares of black and darker pink paper

3-inch (7.6-cm) square of lightweight red paper

Red fine-line felt tip pen

Paper punches, ¹/₈-inch (0.3-cm) and ¹/₄-inch (0.6-cm) diameter circles

TRIM-A-TREE CARD

*S*end this work-in-progress Christmas greeting to a child or child-like friend. The chubby little tree is quickly cut from foil board, and it's fun for the recipient to decorate it with gold sticky-star trimmings. For variety, omit the sticker sheet, cut the tree card from plain sturdy paper, and glue a piece of pretty patterned paper to the front.

❄

1   Photocopy or trace the patterns and cut them out.

2   Score and fold the foil board in half crosswise. Tape the edges together. Align the "place on fold" edge of the tree pattern on the folded edge of the foil board. Anchor the pattern with removable tape, draw around the shape, and cut it out. If you wish, use a stylus or a dull table knife to make horizontal lines between the tiers of the tree.

3   From the red paper, cut two 1½-inch (3.8-cm) squares and glue them together with the foil on the outside. When dry, mark one heart on the double foil, cut it out, and glue it in place on the tree top. If the heart does not stick well, anchor it with tape on the back of the card. Use the remaining square of foil to cut one pot and glue it in place on the card.

MATERIALS

For one 3⁹⁄₁₆- by 5¹⁄₂-inch (9.0- by 14.0-cm) card

Patterns on page 124

3¾- by 11-inch (9.5- by 27.9-cm) piece of foil board for tree

1¹⁄₂- by 4¹⁄₂-inch (3.8- by 11.4-cm) piece of foil paper for heart

Foil star sticker sheet

Envelope, 4³⁄₈ by 5³⁄₄ inches (11.1 by 14.6 cm), or Envelope B pattern, page 88, and instructions, pages 86 to 87

PEACE DOVE

A little extra skill is required to make this peaceful paper dove. Exchange the olive branch for a heart to create a graceful symbol for weddings, anniversaries, and other occasions.

❄

1 Trace or preferably photocopy the patterns but do not cut them out. Trim the pattern paper to an 8-inch (20.3-cm) square.

2 Stack and align the papers in this order, from the bottom: transfer paper, transfer surface up; dove paper, right side up; transfer paper, transfer surface down; pattern, right side up.

3 Firmly draw on all of the pattern lines and the markings. Remove the pattern and transfer papers.

4 Before cutting the individual pieces, lightly score the broken lines on the right side of the body, as well as the outermost curved broken line on the wings. Flip the dove paper to the reverse side and lightly score only the oval shape on the wing piece.

5 Cut the slots on the body. Cut out all of the pieces on the outlines.

6 Place the dove pieces right side up on your work surface. Bend the body sides down along the scored lines. Curl the tail somewhat by pulling it gently over a straightedge. Insert the tail in the rear slot in the body. If it is not a snug fit, tape the tail under the body.

7 On the wings, reinforce each side of the notched area with small pieces of tape placed on the reverse side. Bend down the outer wing sections along the scored lines. Bend up the inner wing sections around the center oval.

8 Carefully slip the notched front of the wing oval into the front slot in the body. Gently push the wings forward in the slot so the oval rises and curves slightly. Insert the wing tab into the middle slot on the body and flatten it against the underbody.

9 Make a pinhole at each X on the wings. Pass the monofilament through the space between the wings and the body, bringing the ends up through the wing holes. Knot the monofilament ends together.

10 To make the optional heart or olive branch, trace your chosen pattern and cut it out. Draw around the pattern on your selected paper and cut out the shape. If cut on folded paper, the heart can carry a message inside. The branch can be curled a little by pulling it across a straightedge. Cut a tiny slot in the beak and insert the heart or branch.

MATERIALS

For one 2- by 5- by 6-inch (5.1- by 12.7- by 15.2-cm) dove

Patterns on page 126

8-inch (20.3-cm) square of sturdy paper

Two 8-inch (20.3-cm) squares of erasable transfer paper

Paper punch, 1/8-inch (0.3-cm) diameter

2- by 3-inch (5.1- by 7.6-cm) piece of sturdy paper for heart or olive branch, optional

26-inch (66.0-cm) length of monofilament

BOW NAPKIN RING

Without using a drop of glue, the ends of a single strip of paper can be softly folded and interlocked to form a bow napkin ring. This is a quick and pretty way to giftwrap each place setting at a winter party or any other seasonal celebrations throughout the year.

❄

1 The pattern on page 124 is only a pattern segment. To make the full pattern, trace two identical pattern segments with all the markings and cut out each one. Before joining them together, refer to drawing 1. Reverse one section by flipping it over, front to back and top to bottom, so the combined unit of pattern sections has two slots on the top edge and the two slots on bottom. Tape the pattern sections together on the dotted center line.

2 Tape or clip the pattern onto your paper and draw around it, using a pin to transfer the slot positions. Remove the pattern and cut out the napkin ring and the slots.

3 Referring to drawing 2, softly fold the ring while aligning the slots to create the bow loops. Overlap the loops, keeping them outside the ring, and interlock the slots at the center front.

1. JOIN REVERSED PATTERN SECTIONS TO MAKE COMPLETE PATTERN.

2. SOFTLY FOLD AND ASSEMBLE RING.

MATERIALS
For one 1 3/4-inch (4.4-cm) napkin ring

Pattern on page 124

1 1/2- by 15-inch (3.8- by 38.1-cm) piece of sturdy paper

ENVELOPES

Creating your own envelopes is truly a quick and easy task once you have drawn the patterns. It's also fun because of the unlimited choices of color, texture, and size. Patterns and illustrated instructions are provided here for making five envelope sizes. To make an envelope of a different size, carefully lift the glued flap of an existing envelope, open the folds, and use the flattened envelope as a pattern to create others. Glue your envelope patterns to acetate to extend their lives.

In order to be acceptable for mailing, envelopes must conform to certain postal standards regarding minimum size, proper height-to-length ratio, and maximum thickness of contents. To avoid postal surcharges as well as delivery delays due to returned unacceptable envelopes, visit your post office and request information about current standards or ask for a photocopy of the template that clerks use to check mail dimensions. At the time of writing, all of the envelopes in this book meet the United States Postal Service requirements.

MATERIALS

For one envelope A, B, C, D, or E

**Pattern size of your choice,
pages 87 to 89**

**Paper of your choice (size
requirements listed on each
pattern)**

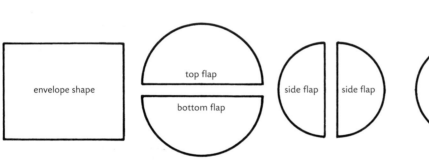

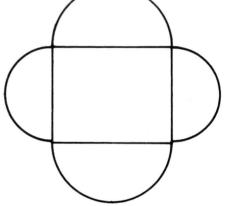

1. TRACE RECTANGULAR ENVELOPE PATTERN IN SIZE OF YOUR CHOICE. ALSO MAKE TWO TRACINGS OF SEMICIRCULAR TOP/BOTTOM FLAP AND TWO TRACINGS OF SEMICIRCULAR SIDE FLAP. FOR GREATEST ACCURACY, USE A COMPASS TO TRACE SEMICIRCLES. CUT OUT ALL PATTERN PIECES.

2. ARRANGE PATTERN PIECES IN PROPER ORDER ON WORK SURFACE AND TAPE TOGETHER. PRACTICE FOLDING ENVELOPE PATTERN TO CHECK ALIGNMENT OF FLAPS.

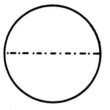

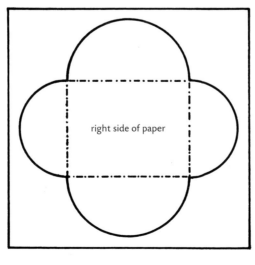

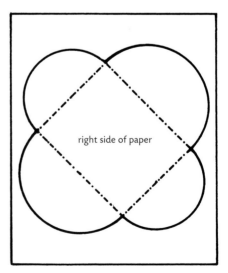

3. TRACE PATTERN FOR OPTIONAL LINER CIRCLE ON FOLDED PAPER AND CUT OUT.

4. PLACE SQUARE OR RECTANGLE OF SELECTED PAPER RIGHT SIDE UP ON WORK SURFACE. TAPE OR CLIP PATTERN ONTO PAPER AND DRAW AROUND PATTERN SHAPE. REMOVE PATTERN. DRAW AND SCORE PERPENDICULAR LINES WITHIN OUTLINED SHAPE TO DEFINE STRAIGHT EDGES OF ENVELOPE. CUT OUT SHAPE.

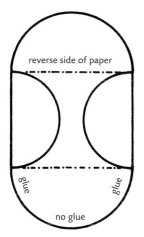

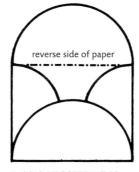

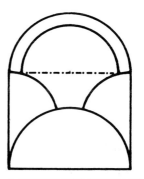

5. FLIP ENVELOPE OVER TO REVERSE SIDE OF PAPER. FOLD IN SIDE FLAPS. APPLY GLUE TO EDGES OF BOTTOM FLAP, AVOIDING CENTER AREA.

6. FOLD UP BOTTOM FLAP SO IT OVERLAPS SIDE FLAPS. TO PROTECT INTERIOR OF ENVELOPE FROM MISPLACED GLUE, SLIDE IN A PIECE OF SCRAP PAPER TO KEEP FRONT AND BACK LAYERS SEPARATED. REMOVE SCRAP PAPER JUST BEFORE GLUE IS DRY.

7. FLIP OPTIONAL LINER OVER TO REVERSE SIDE AND APPLY GLUE ONLY TO HALF OF CIRCLE ABOVE FOLDING LINE.

8. SLIDE UNGLUED PORTION OF LINER INSIDE ENVELOPE. CENTER GLUED AREA OF LINER ON TOP FLAP, ALIGNING FOLDS, AND PRESS LAYERS TOGETHER. IMMEDIATELY FOLD DOWN TOP FLAP TO FINALIZE PLACEMENT OF LINER. IN ORDER TO HINGE WELL, FOLDING LINES OF LINER AND ENVELOPE WILL PROBABLY SHIFT AND NOT BE ALIGNED AFTER FOLDING DOWN AND THEN LIFTING TOP FLAP. INSERT CARD AND SEAL ENVELOPE.

ENVELOPE A

Final size: 4 1/0 by 5 1/2 inches (10.5 by 14.0 cm)
Paper size: 10-inch (25.4-cm) square or 8 1/2- by 11-inch (21.6- by 27.9-cm) rectangle

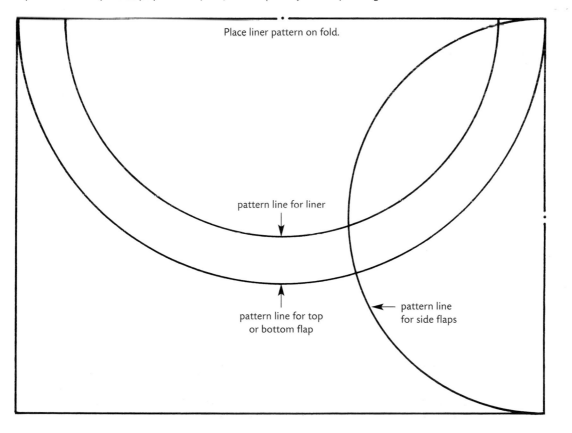

Place liner pattern on fold.

pattern line for liner

pattern line for top or bottom flap

pattern line for side flaps

ENVELOPE B

Final size: 4³/₈ by
5³/₄ inches
(11.1 by 14.6 cm)
Paper size: 10¹/₂-inch
(26.7-cm) square
or 9- by 12-inch
(22.9- by 30.5-cm)
rectangle

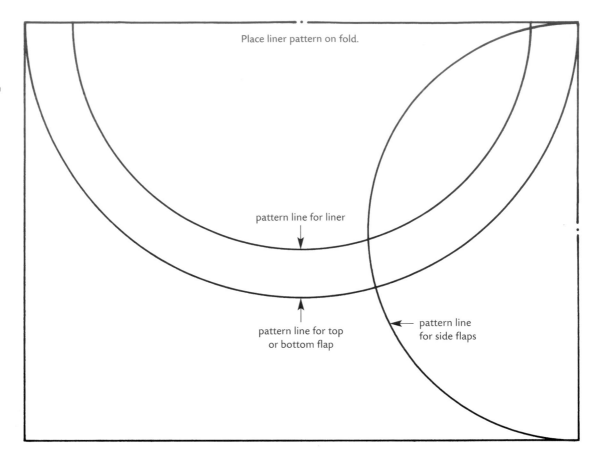

Place liner pattern on fold.

pattern line for liner

pattern line for top
or bottom flap

pattern line
for side flaps

ENVELOPE C

Final size: 4¹/₄ by 5¹/₈ inches
(10.8 by 13.0 cm)
Paper size: 9³/₄-inch (24.8-cm)
square or 8¹/₂- by 11-inch
(21.6- by 27.9-cm) rectangle

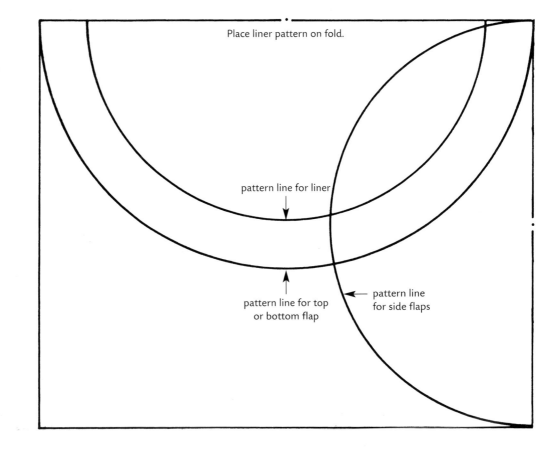

Place liner pattern on fold.

pattern line for liner

pattern line for top
or bottom flap

pattern line
for side flaps

ENVELOPE D

Final size: 3 5/8 by 6 1/2 inches (9.2 by 16.5 cm)
Paper size: 10 1/2-inch (26.7-cm) square or 9- by 12-inch (22.9- by 30.5-cm) rectangle

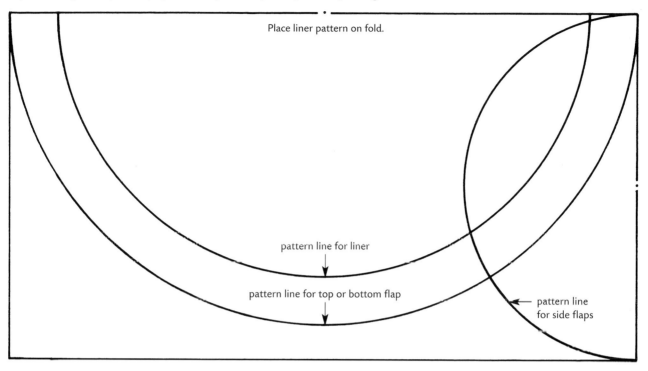

Place liner pattern on fold.

pattern line for liner

pattern line for top or bottom flap

pattern line
for side flaps

ENVELOPE E

Final size: 3 7/8 by 5 3/8 inches (9.8 by 13.6 cm)
Paper size: 9 1/2 inch (24.1 cm) square or 8 1/2- by 11-inch (21.6- by 27.9-cm) rectangle

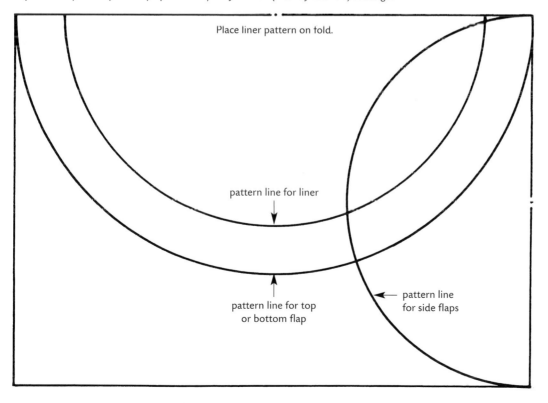

Place liner pattern on fold.

pattern line for liner

pattern line for top
or bottom flap

pattern line
for side flaps

PATTERNS

The patterns in this section are shown full-size, and can be photocopied or traced. Note that solid lines indicate cutting lines, broken lines are folding lines, and dotted lines show placement of a detail or another piece. Page numbers for the complete project instructions are given with each pattern.

HUGS AND KISSES CARD

(Instructions on page 22.)

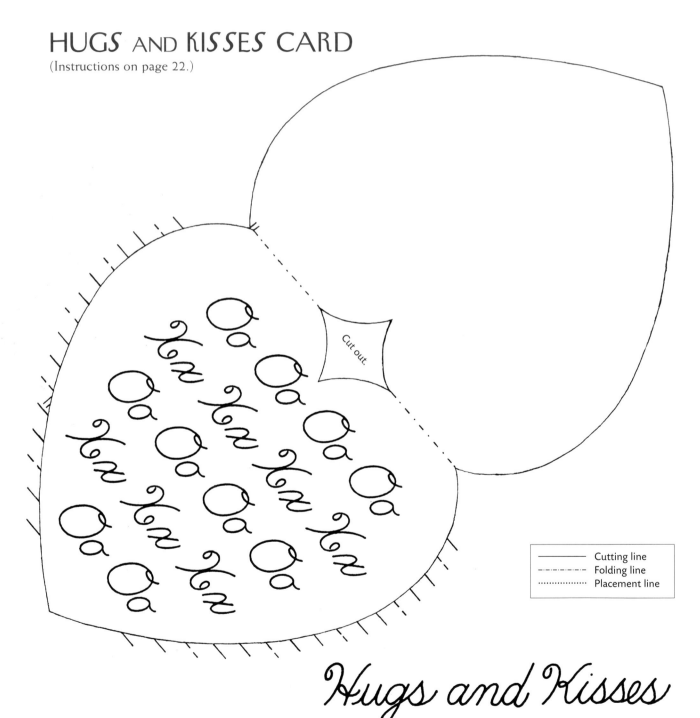

Cut out.

	Cutting line
	Folding line
	Placement line

Hugs and Kisses

Inside Message

PLEATED HEART ORNAMENT

(Instructions on page 24.)

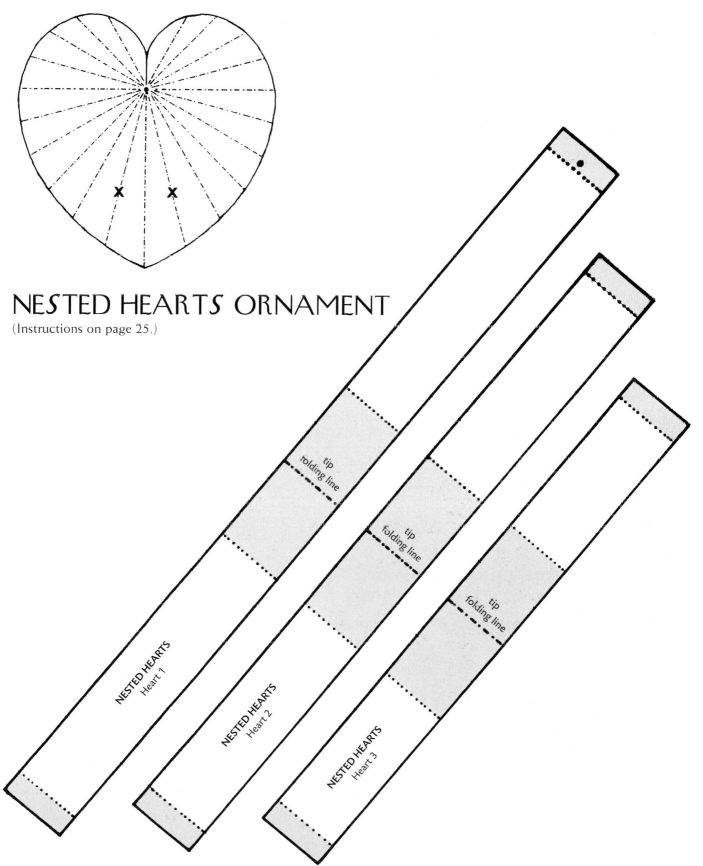

NESTED HEARTS ORNAMENT

(Instructions on page 25.)

NESTED HEARTS
Heart 1

NESTED HEARTS
Heart 2

NESTED HEARTS
Heart 3

tip
folding line

tip
folding line

tip
folding line

CANDY HEART BASKET

(Instructions on page 27.)

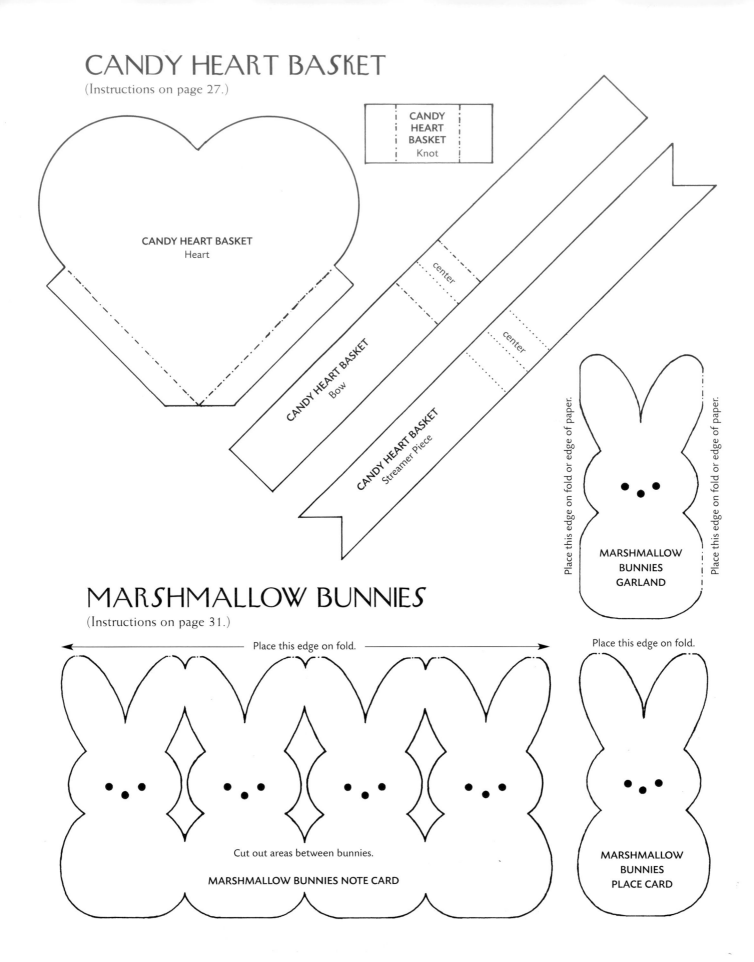

CANDY
HEART
BASKET
Knot

CANDY HEART BASKET
Heart

CANDY HEART BASKET
Bow

center

center

CANDY HEART BASKET
Streamer Piece

Place this edge on fold or edge of paper.

Place this edge on fold or edge of paper.

MARSHMALLOW
BUNNIES
GARLAND

MARSHMALLOW BUNNIES

(Instructions on page 31.)

Place this edge on fold.

Place this edge on fold.

Cut out areas between bunnies.

MARSHMALLOW BUNNIES NOTE CARD

MARSHMALLOW
BUNNIES
PLACE CARD

TOY KEYS CARD

(Instructions on page 30.)

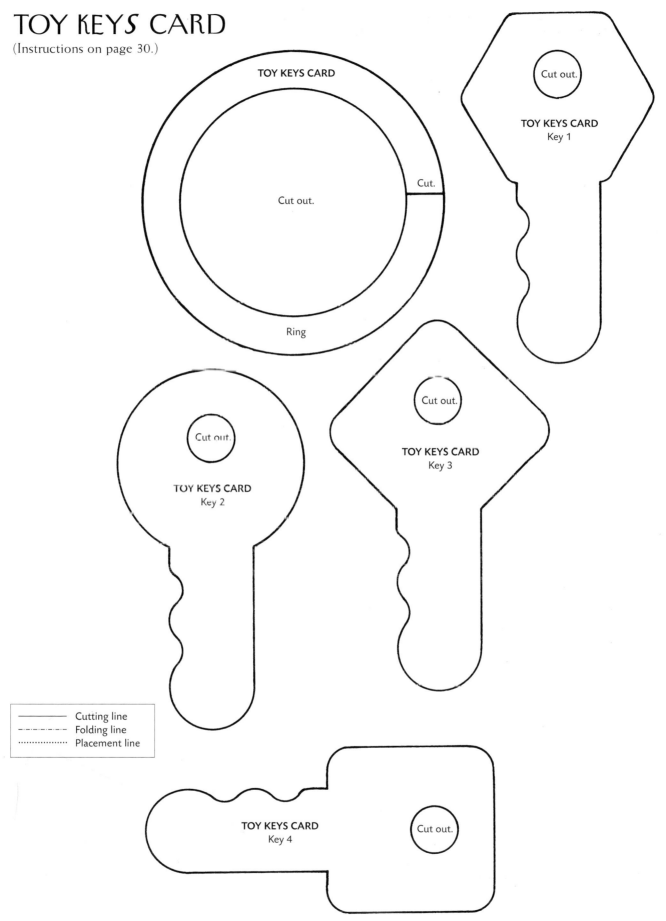

TOY KEYS CARD

Cut out.

Cut.

Ring

TOY KEYS CARD
Key 1

Cut out.

TOY KEYS CARD
Key 2

Cut out.

TOY KEYS CARD
Key 3

Cut out.

Cutting line
Folding line
Placement line

TOY KEYS CARD
Key 4

Cut out.

CROSS CARDS
(Instructions on pages 32–33.)

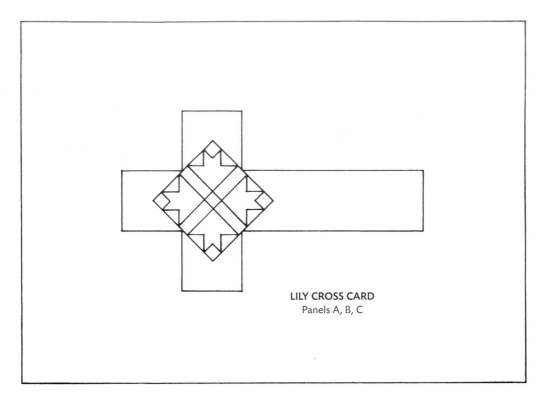

LILY CROSS CARD
Panels A, B, C

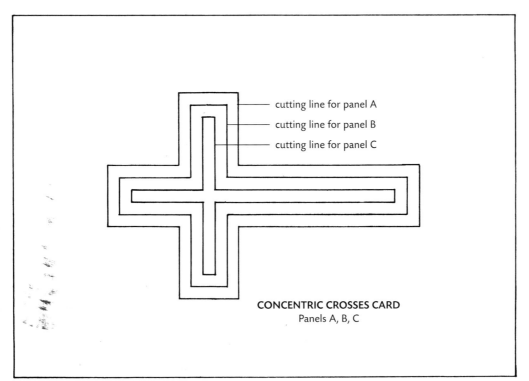

cutting line for panel A
cutting line for panel B
cutting line for panel C

CONCENTRIC CROSSES CARD
Panels A, B, C

CROSS CARDS

(continued)

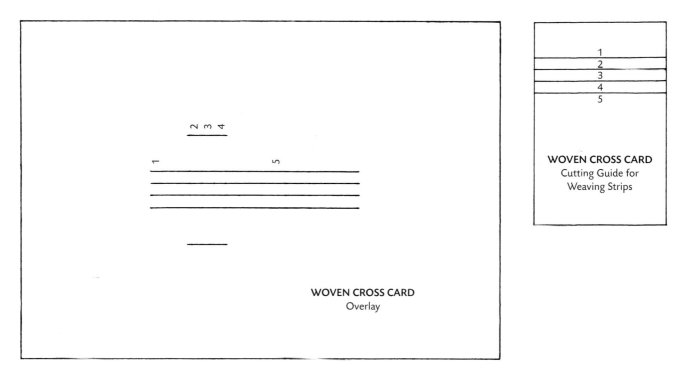

WOVEN CROSS CARD
Overlay

WOVEN CROSS CARD
Cutting Guide for
Weaving Strips

BABY BOOTIES

(Instructions on pages 28 29.)

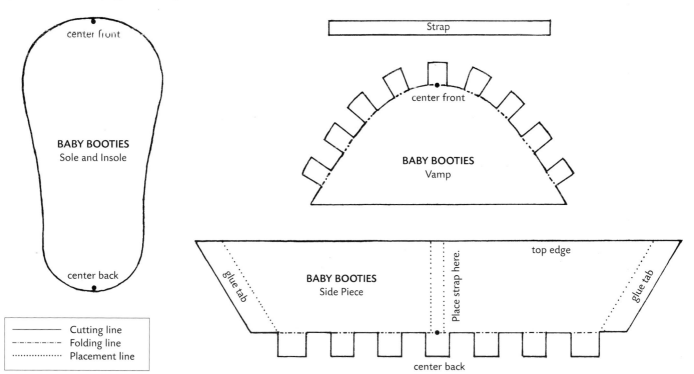

center front

BABY BOOTIES
Sole and Insole

center back

Strap

center front

BABY BOOTIES
Vamp

top edge

BABY BOOTIES
Side Piece

glue tab

Place strap here.

glue tab

center back

———— Cutting line
—·—·—·— Folding line
················ Placement line

SPRINGTIME HATS AND BOXES

(Instructions on pages 34–35.)

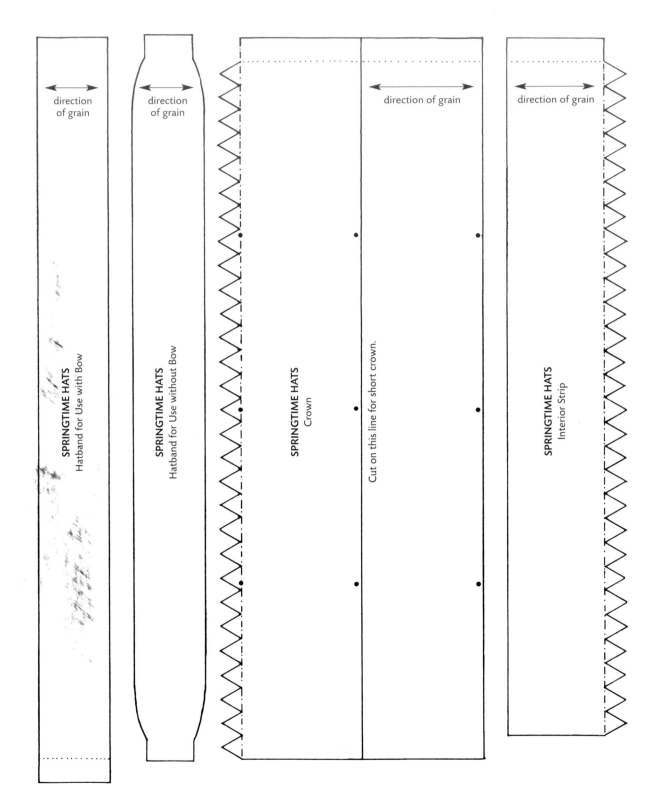

SPRINGTIME HATS
Hatband for Use with Bow

direction of grain

SPRINGTIME HATS
Hatband for Use without Bow

direction of grain

SPRINGTIME HATS
Crown

direction of grain

Cut on this line for short crown.

SPRINGTIME HATS
Interior Strip

direction of grain

SPRINGTIME HATS AND BOXES

(continued)

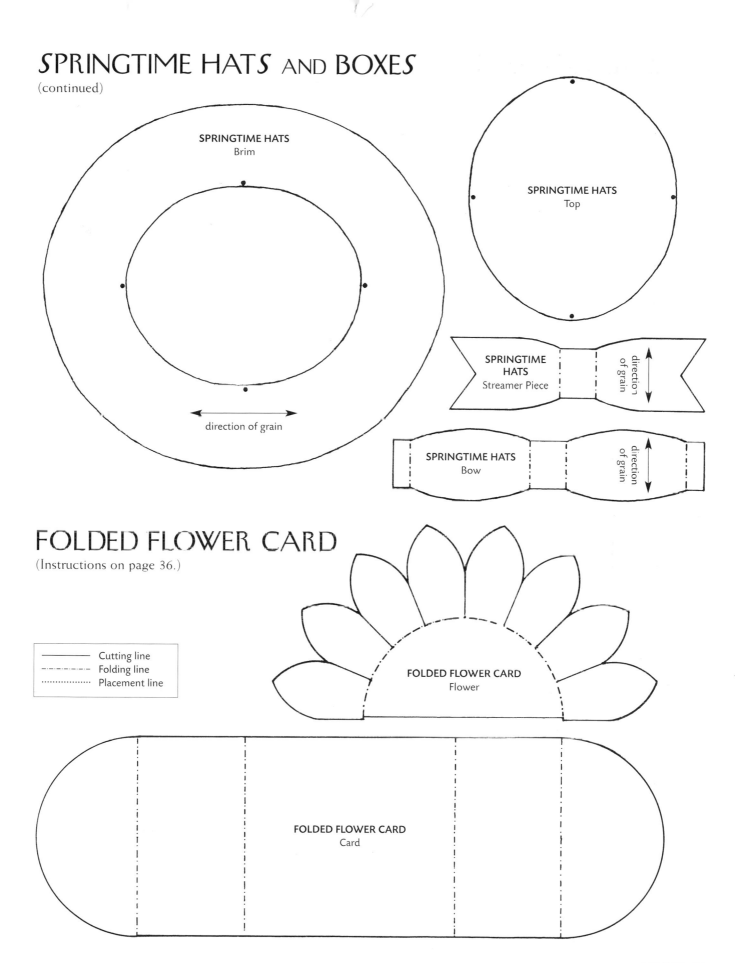

SPRINGTIME HATS
Brim

direction of grain

SPRINGTIME HATS
Top

SPRINGTIME HATS
Streamer Piece

direction of grain

SPRINGTIME HATS
Bow

direction of grain

FOLDED FLOWER CARD

(Instructions on page 36.)

———— Cutting line
—·—·—· Folding line
·············· Placement line

FOLDED FLOWER CARD
Flower

FOLDED FLOWER CARD
Card

SPRING NAPKIN RINGS

(Instructions on page 37.)

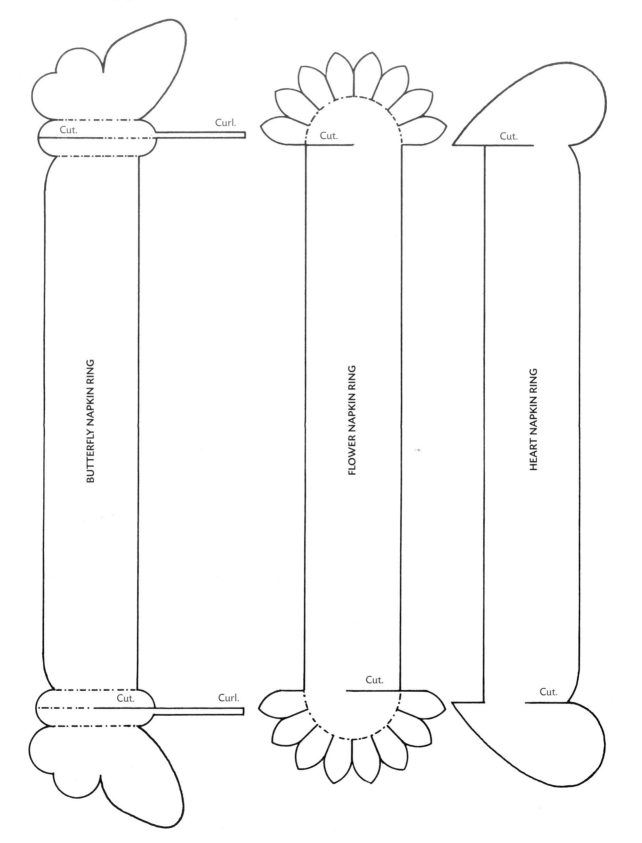

LEMONADE CARD

(Instructions on page 40.)

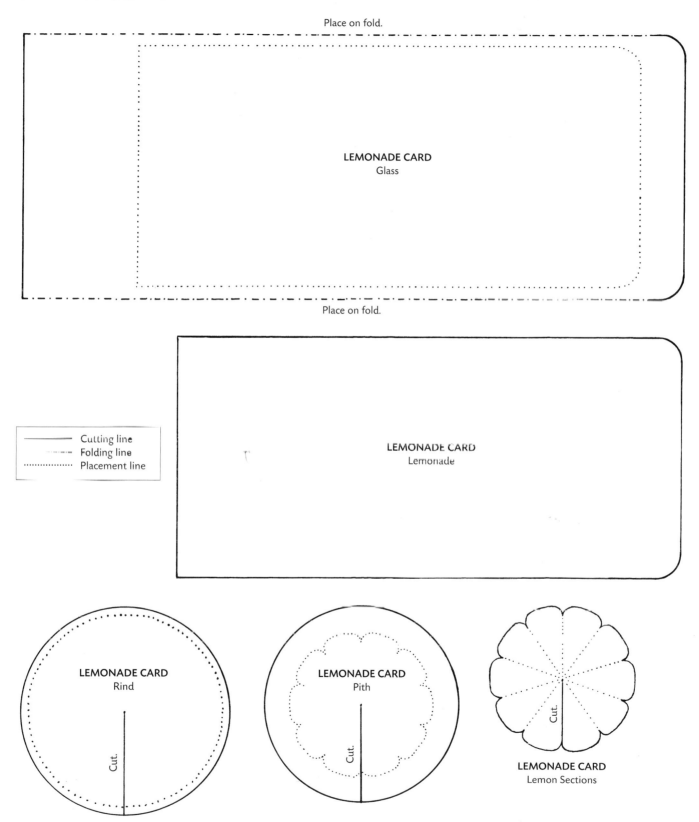

Place on fold.

LEMONADE CARD
Glass

Place on fold.

Cutting line
Folding line
Placement line

LEMONADE CARD
Lemonade

LEMONADE CARD
Rind

Cut.

LEMONADE CARD
Pith

Cut.

Cut.

LEMONADE CARD
Lemon Sections

FRUIT BASKETS

(Instructions on page 41.)

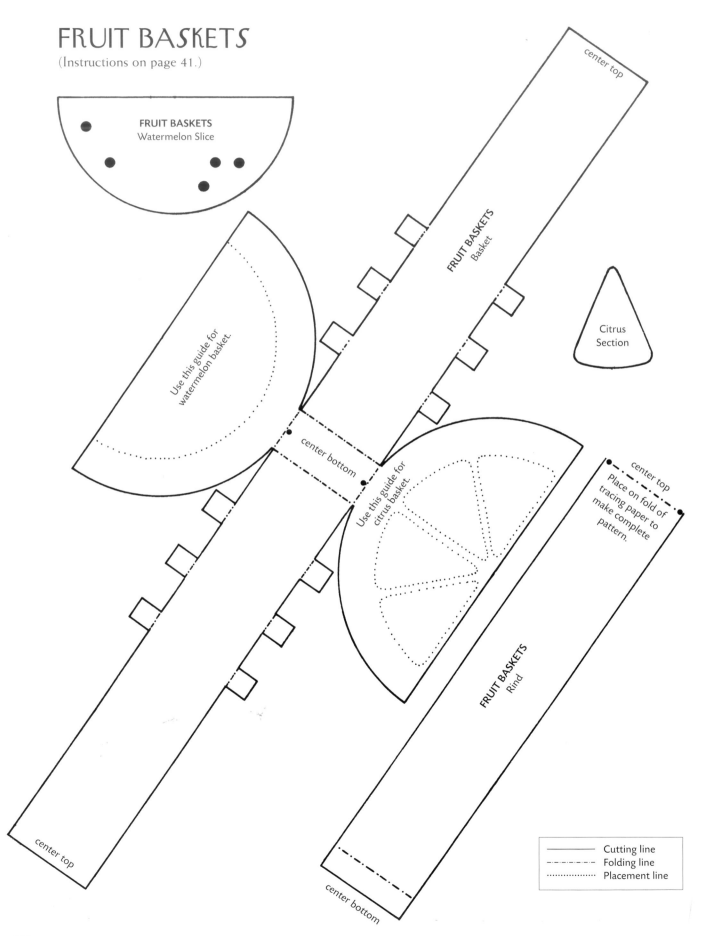

FRUIT BASKETS
Watermelon Slice

FRUIT BASKETS
Basket

Citrus Section

Use this guide for watermelon basket.

center bottom

Use this guide for citrus basket.

center top

Place on fold of tracing paper to make complete pattern.

FRUIT BASKETS
Rind

center top

center bottom

———	Cutting line
—·—·—	Folding line
··········	Placement line

GARDEN GLOVES GIFT CARD

(Instructions on page 42.)

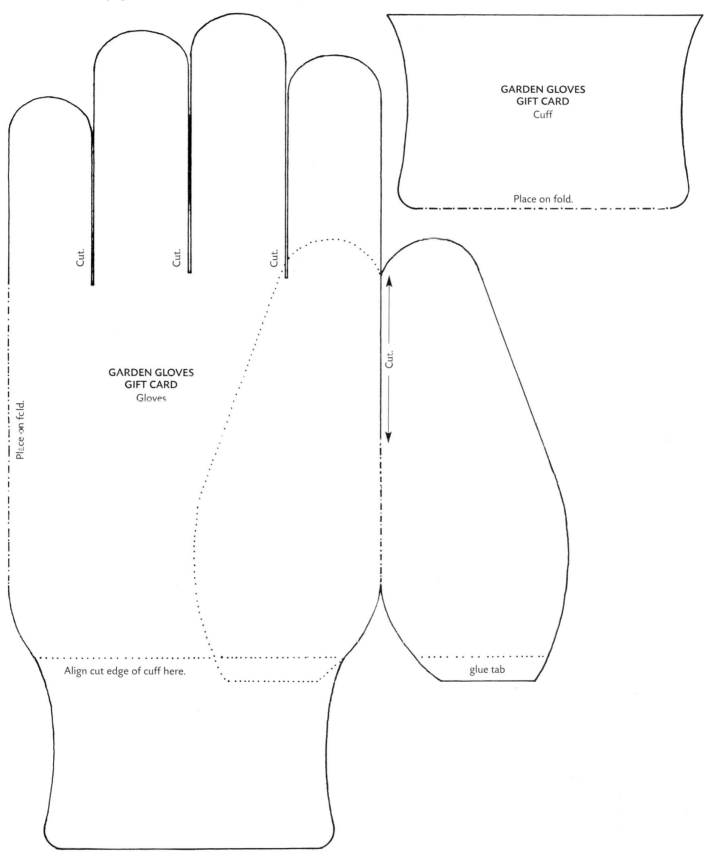

GARDEN GLOVES
GIFT CARD
Cuff

Place on fold.

Cut.

Cut.

Cut.

Place on fold.

GARDEN GLOVES
GIFT CARD
Gloves

Cut.

Align cut edge of cuff here.

glue tab

CLASSIC SUMMER TOTE

(Instructions on page 43.)

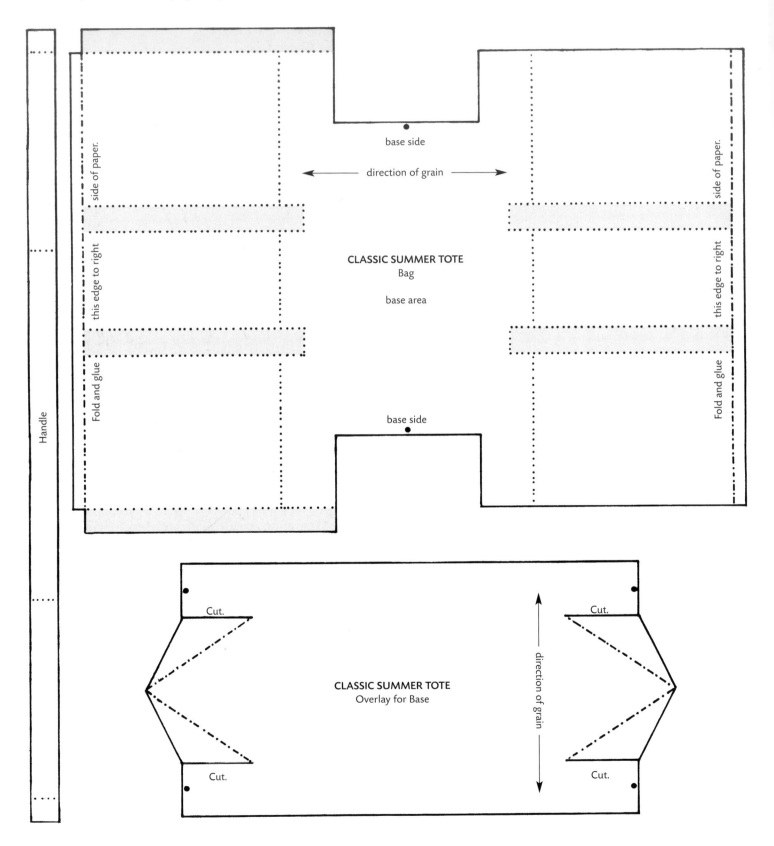

CLASSIC SUMMER TOTE
Bag

base area

base side

direction of grain

side of paper.

this edge to right

Fold and glue

Handle

CLASSIC SUMMER TOTE
Overlay for Base

direction of grain

Cut.

PARTY HAT

(Instructions on page 44.)

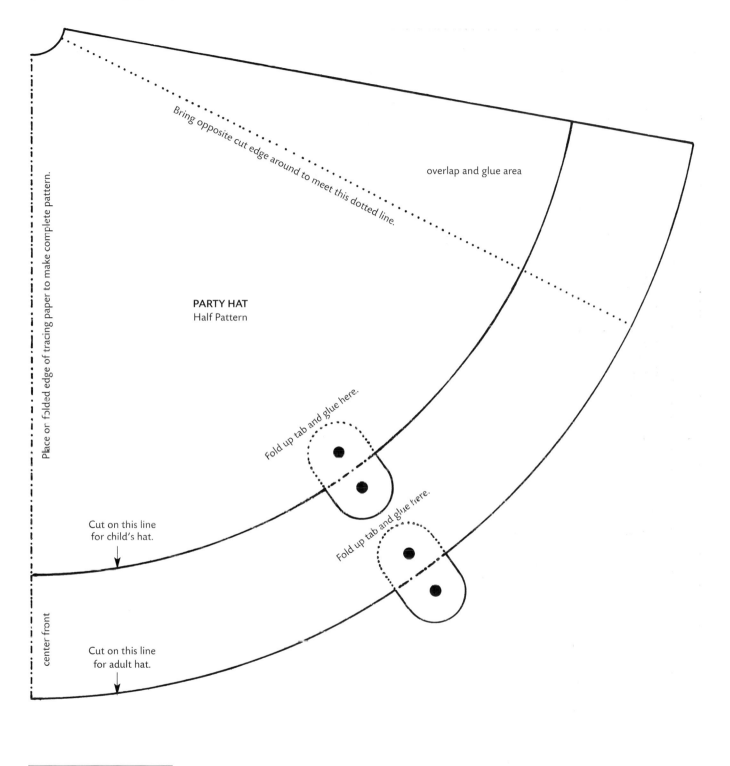

Bring opposite cut edge around to meet this dotted line.

overlap and glue area

Place or folded edge of tracing paper to make complete pattern.

PARTY HAT
Half Pattern

Fold up tab and glue here.

Fold up tab and glue here.

Cut on this line
for child's hat.

center front

Cut on this line
for adult hat.

——————— Cutting line
—·—·—·—·— Folding line
················ Placement line

SIMPLE STAR

(Instructions on page 45.)

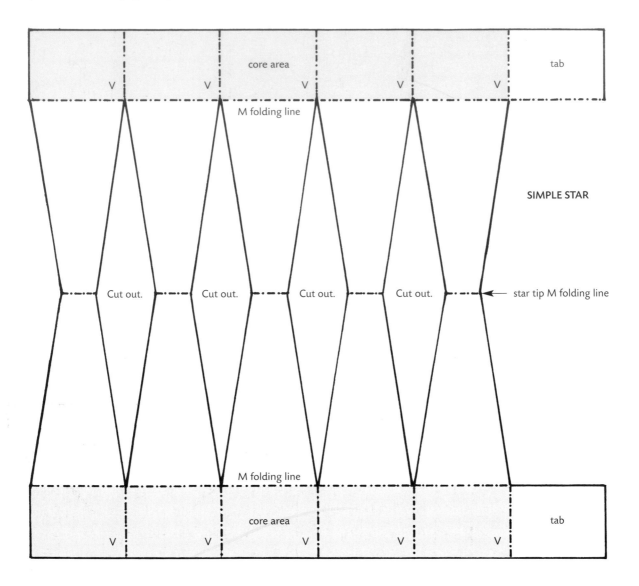

core area

tab

V   V   V   V   V

M folding line

SIMPLE STAR

Cut out.   Cut out.   Cut out.   Cut out.   ← star tip M folding line

M folding line

core area

tab

V   V   V   V   V

STENCIL GIFT TAG

(Instructions on page 48.)

STENCIL GIFT TAG

	Cutting line
	Folding line
	Placement line

TWIN POP NOTES

(Instructions on page 46.)

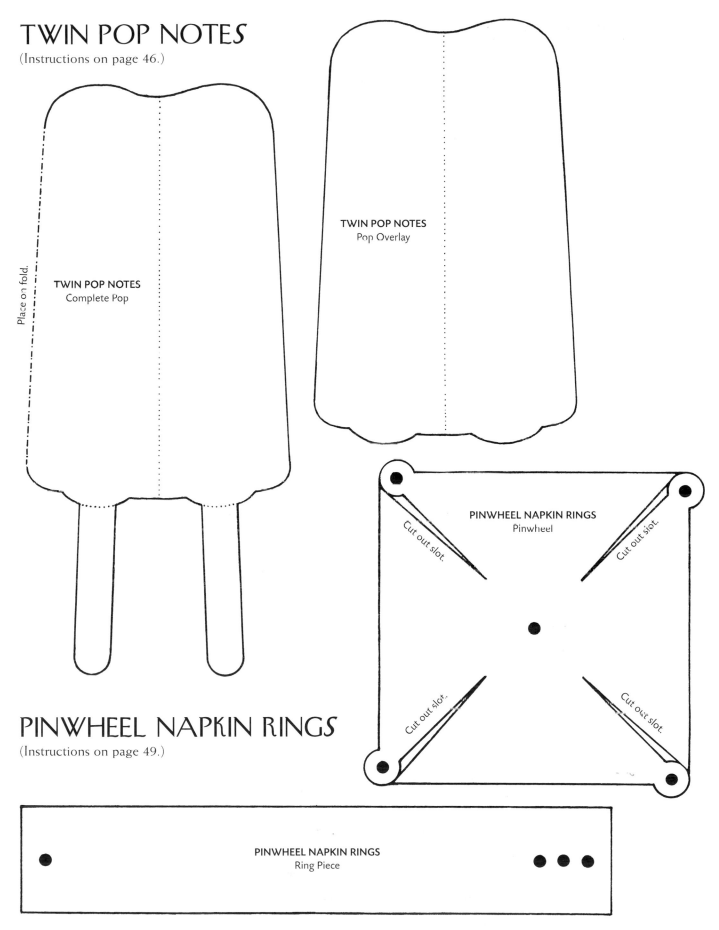

TWIN POP NOTES
Complete Pop

Place on fold.

TWIN POP NOTES
Pop Overlay

PINWHEEL NAPKIN RINGS
Pinwheel

Cut out slot.

Cut out slot.

Cut out slot.

Cut out slot.

PINWHEEL NAPKIN RINGS

(Instructions on page 49.)

PINWHEEL NAPKIN RINGS
Ring Piece

PIGS AND PIGLETS

(Instructions on page 47.)

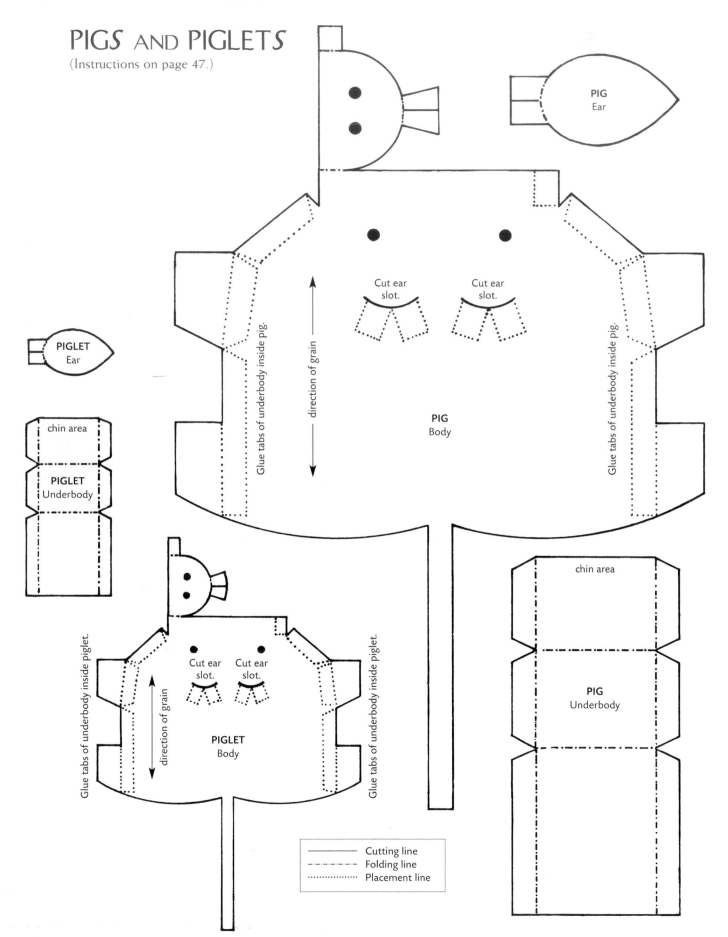

PIG
Ear

PIGLET
Ear

chin area

PIGLET
Underbody

Glue tabs of underbody inside pig.

direction of grain

Cut ear slot.

Cut ear slot.

PIG
Body

Glue tabs of underbody inside pig.

Glue tabs of underbody inside piglet.

direction of grain

Cut ear slot.

Cut ear slot.

PIGLET
Body

Glue tabs of underbody inside piglet.

chin area

PIG
Underbody

	Cutting line
	Folding line
	Placement line

SUMMER TEE SET

(Instructions on pages 50–51.)

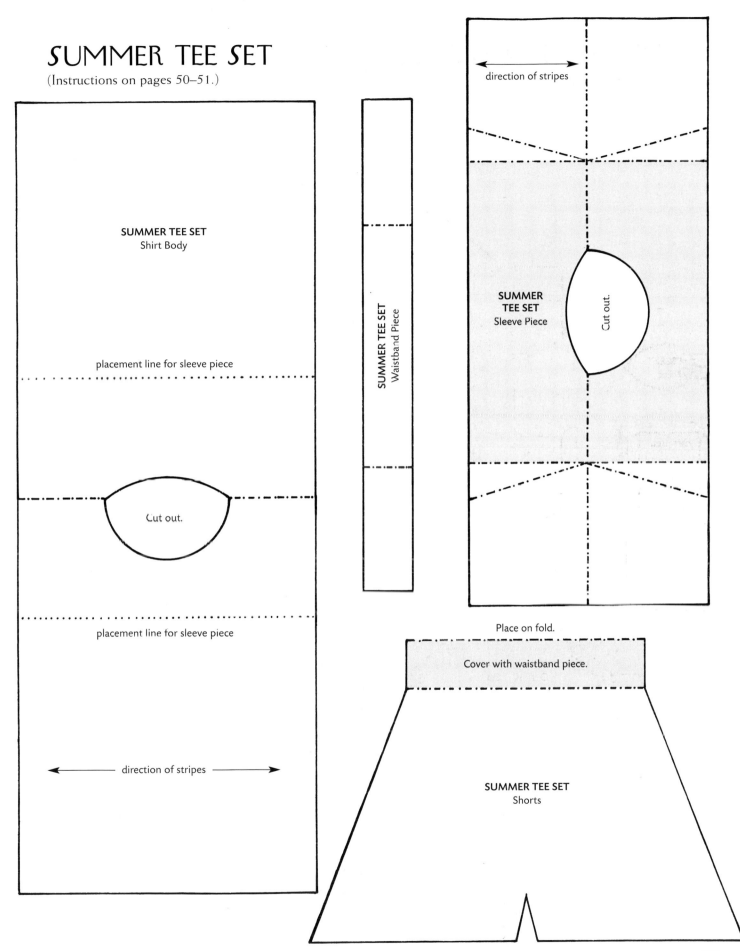

direction of stripes

SUMMER TEE SET
Shirt Body

placement line for sleeve piece

Cut out.

placement line for sleeve piece

← direction of stripes →

SUMMER TEE SET
Waistband Piece

SUMMER TEE SET
Sleeve Piece

Cut out.

Place on fold.

Cover with waistband piece.

SUMMER TEE SET
Shorts

LEAF GARLAND AND WREATH

(Instructions on pages 54–55.)

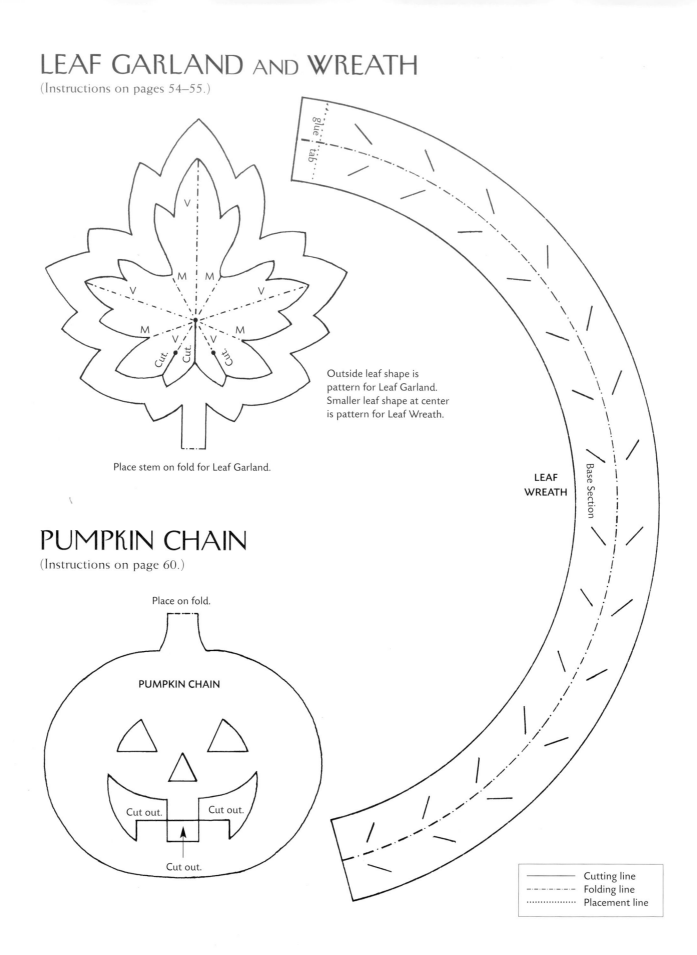

Outside leaf shape is pattern for Leaf Garland. Smaller leaf shape at center is pattern for Leaf Wreath.

Place stem on fold for Leaf Garland.

PUMPKIN CHAIN

(Instructions on page 60.)

Place on fold.

PUMPKIN CHAIN

Cut out.   Cut out.

Cut out.

glue tab

LEAF WREATH   Base Section

	Cutting line
	Folding line
	Placement line

SQUIRREL NOTE AND GARLAND

(Instructions on pages 56–57.)

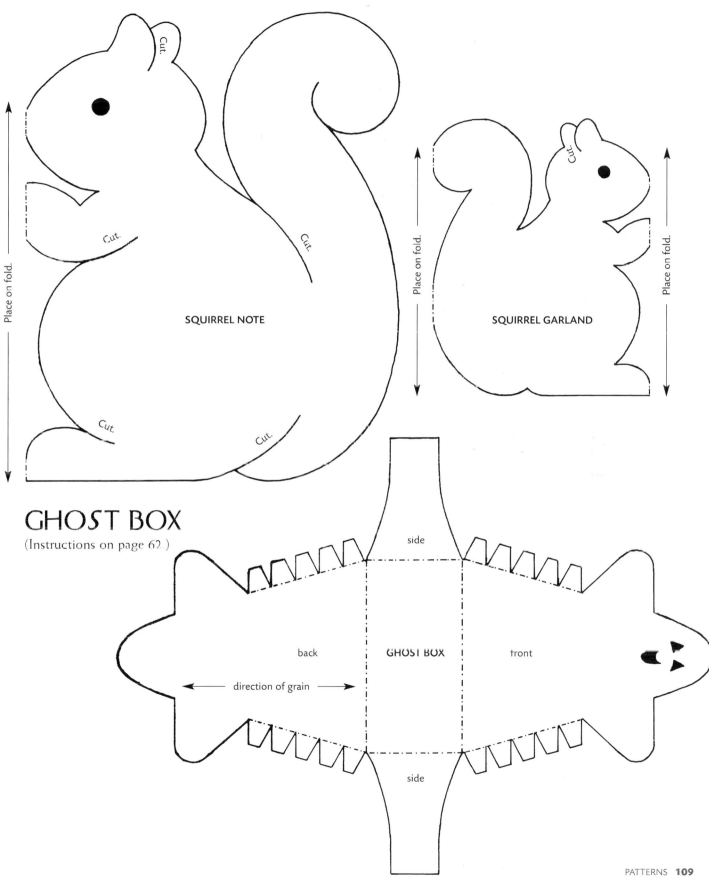

SQUIRREL NOTE

Place on fold.

Cut.

Cut.

Cut.

Cut.

SQUIRREL GARLAND

Place on fold.

Place on fold.

Cut.

GHOST BOX

(Instructions on page 62.)

side

back

GHOST BOX

front

direction of grain

side

CURLED STARS

(Instructions on page 59.)

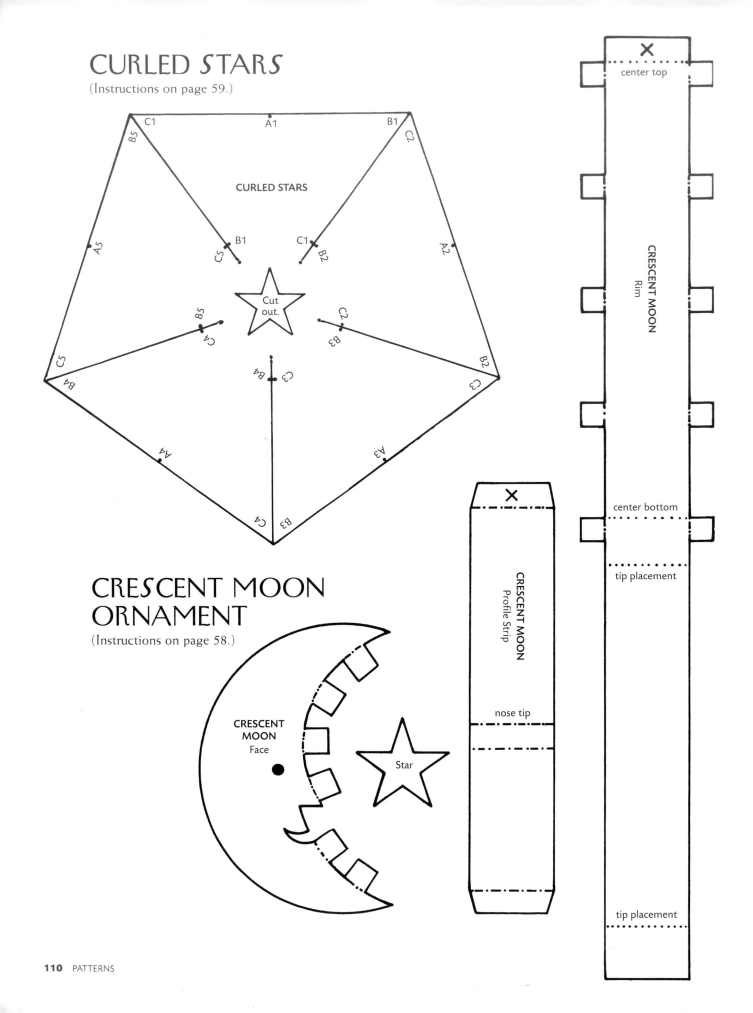

CURLED STARS

Cut out.

CRESCENT MOON ORNAMENT

(Instructions on page 58.)

CRESCENT MOON
Face

Star

CRESCENT MOON
Profile Strip

nose tip

CRESCENT MOON
Rim

center top

center bottom

tip placement

tip placement

BAT WREATH

(Instructions on page 61.)

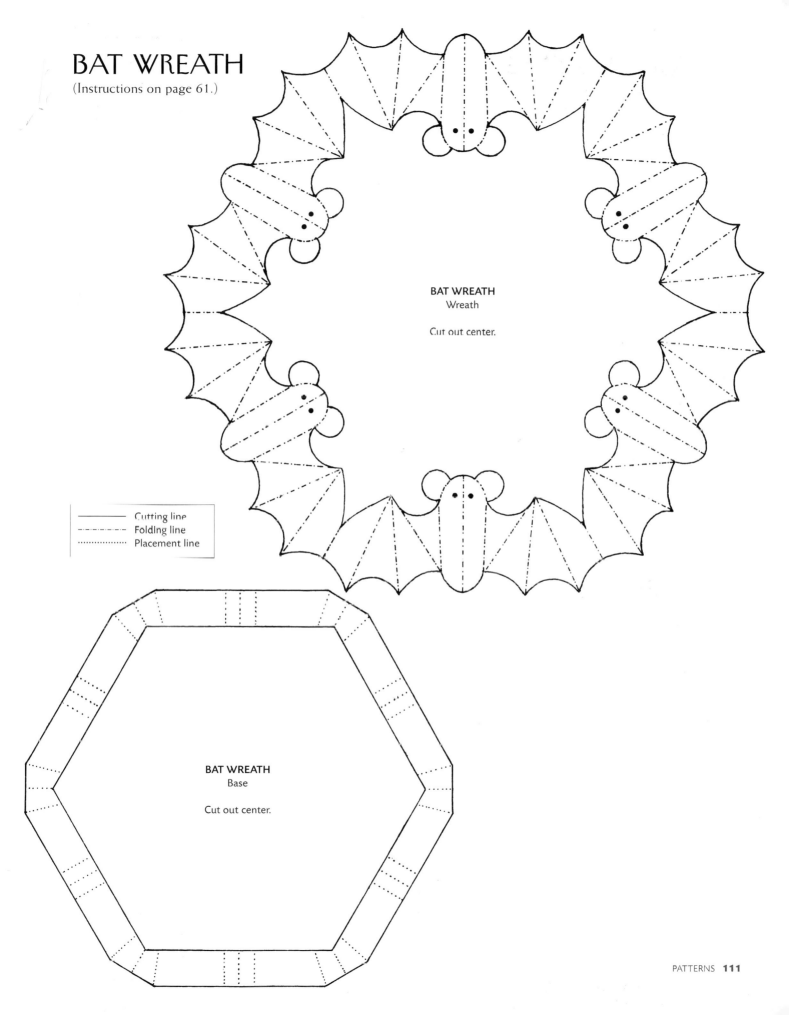

Cutting line
Folding line
Placement line

BAT WREATH
Wreath

Cut out center.

BAT WREATH
Base

Cut out center.

WITCH HAT CORNUCOPIA
(Instructions on page 63.)

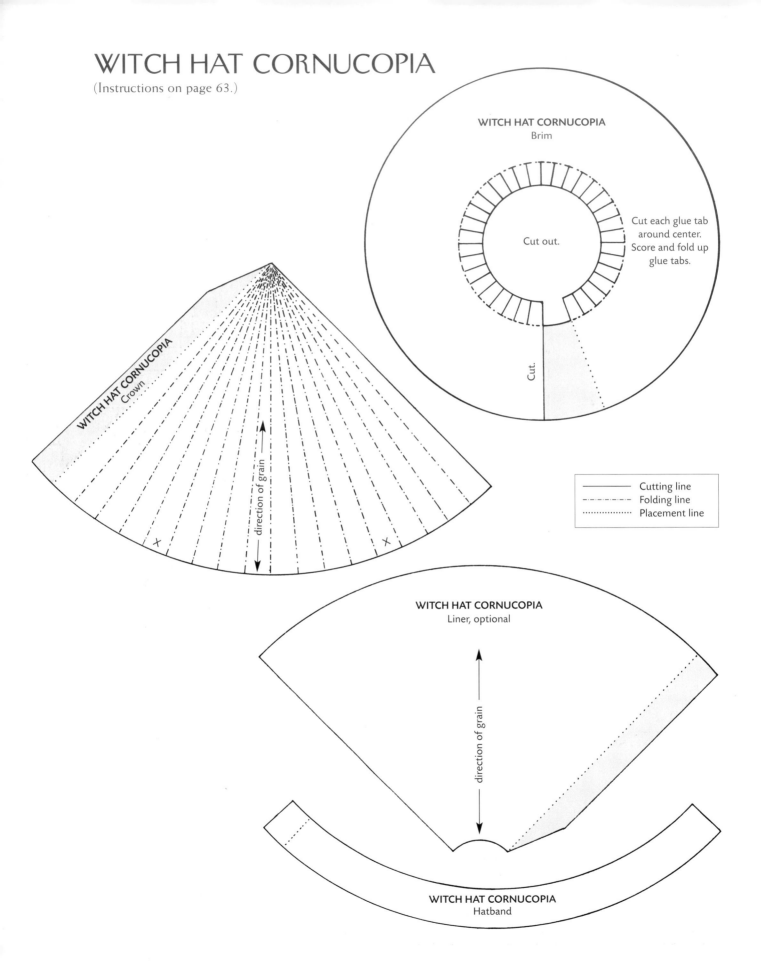

WITCH HAT CORNUCOPIA
Brim

Cut out.

Cut each glue tab around center. Score and fold up glue tabs.

Cut.

WITCH HAT CORNUCOPIA
Crown

direction of grain

X   X

	Cutting line
	Folding line
	Placement line

WITCH HAT CORNUCOPIA
Liner, optional

direction of grain

WITCH HAT CORNUCOPIA
Hatband

TWIN HOUSE CARDS

(Instructions on page 67.)

Place on fold.

TWIN HOUSE
CARDS

PUMPKIN PACKAGES

(Instructions on
pages 64–65.)

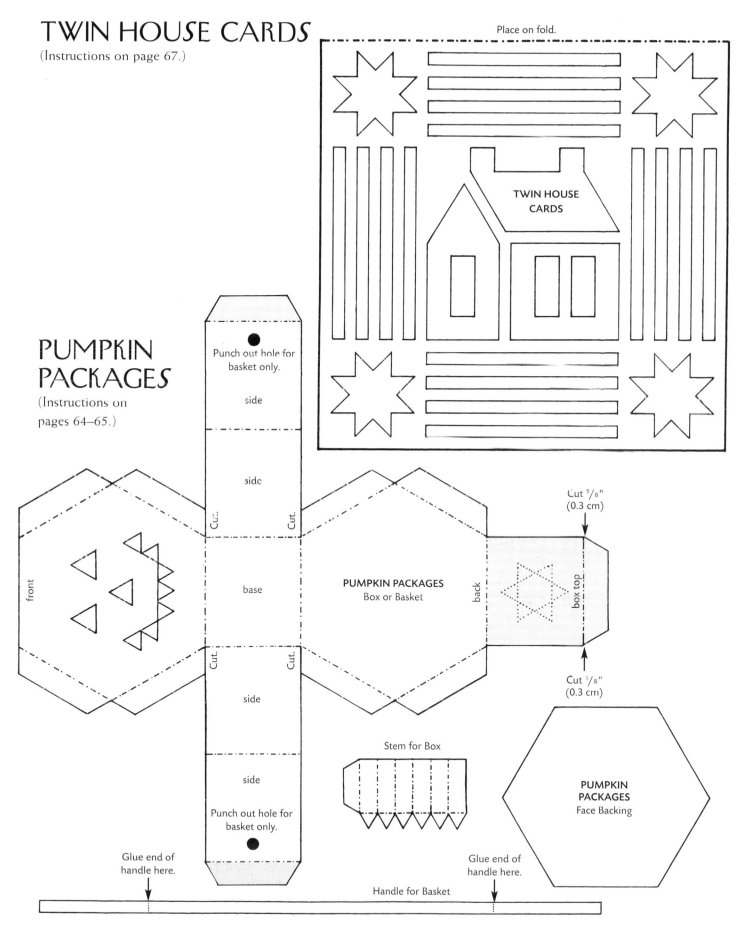

Punch out hole for
basket only.

side

side

Cut.

Cut.

base

side

Cut.

Cut.

side

Punch out hole for
basket only.

front

PUMPKIN PACKAGES
Box or Basket

back

box top

Cut ¹/₈"
(0.3 cm)

Cut ¹/₈"
(0.3 cm)

Stem for Box

PUMPKIN
PACKAGES
Face Backing

Glue end of
handle here.

Glue end of
handle here.

Handle for Basket

CHAIR PLACE CARDS
(Instructions on page 66.)

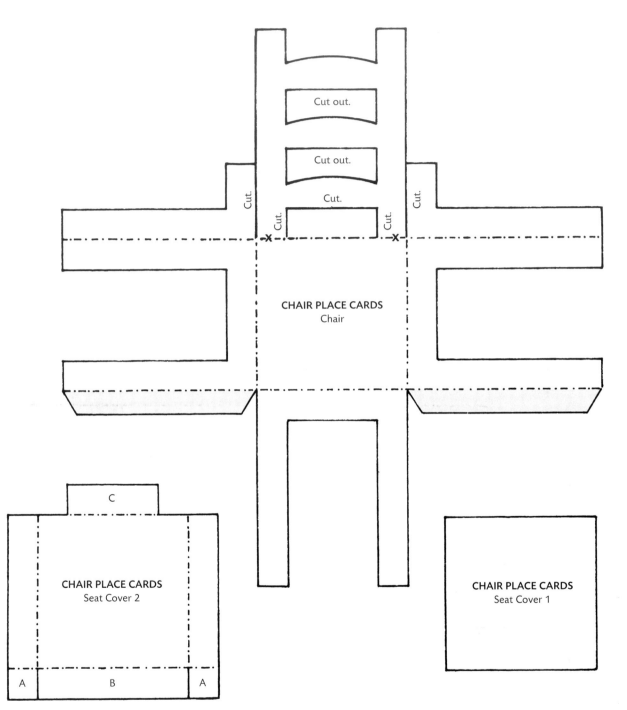

Cut out.

Cut out.

Cut.

Cut.

Cut.

Cut.

Cut.

CHAIR PLACE CARDS
Chair

C

CHAIR PLACE CARDS
Seat Cover 2

A   B   A

CHAIR PLACE CARDS
Seat Cover 1

	Cutting line
	Folding line
	Placement line

COOKIE SHEET BOOK

(Instructions on page 70.)

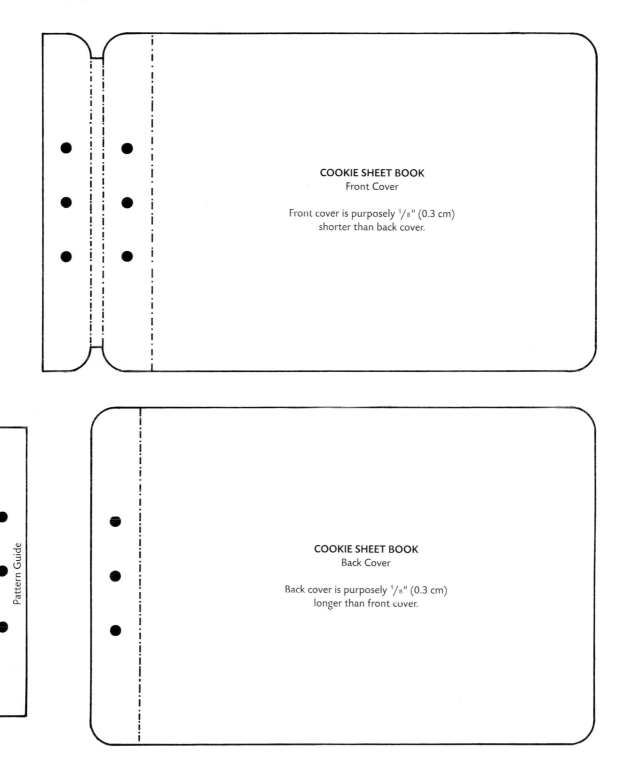

COOKIE SHEET BOOK
Front Cover

Front cover is purposely ¹/₈" (0.3 cm)
shorter than back cover.

COOKIE SHEET BOOK
Pattern Guide

COOKIE SHEET BOOK
Back Cover

Back cover is purposely ¹/₈" (0.3 cm)
longer than front cover.

COCOA CARD

(Instructions on page 71.)

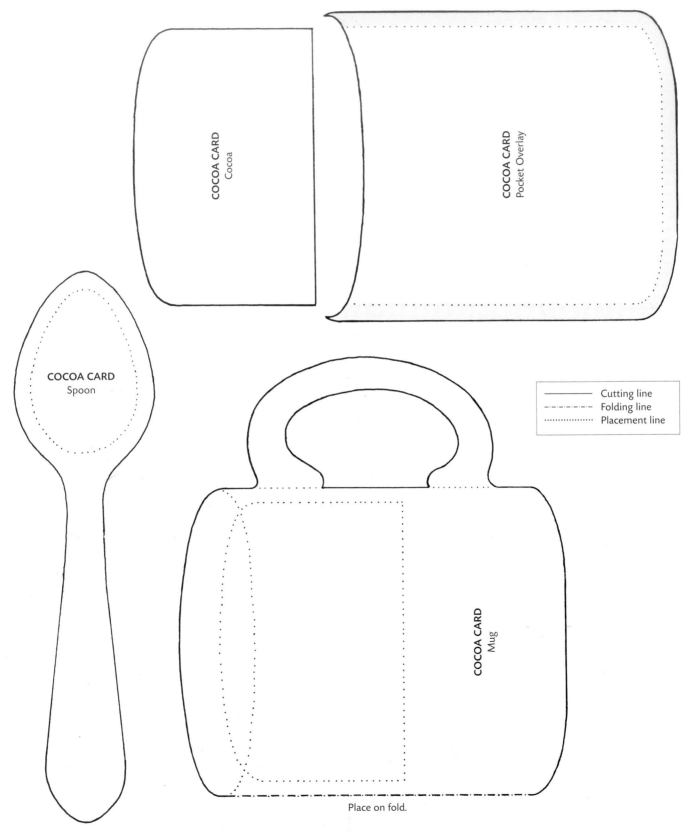

COCOA CARD
Cocoa

COCOA CARD
Pocket Overlay

COCOA CARD
Spoon

COCOA CARD
Mug

Place on fold.

———	Cutting line
—·—·—	Folding line
············	Placement line

FRINGED PINE TREE

(Instructions on page 74.)

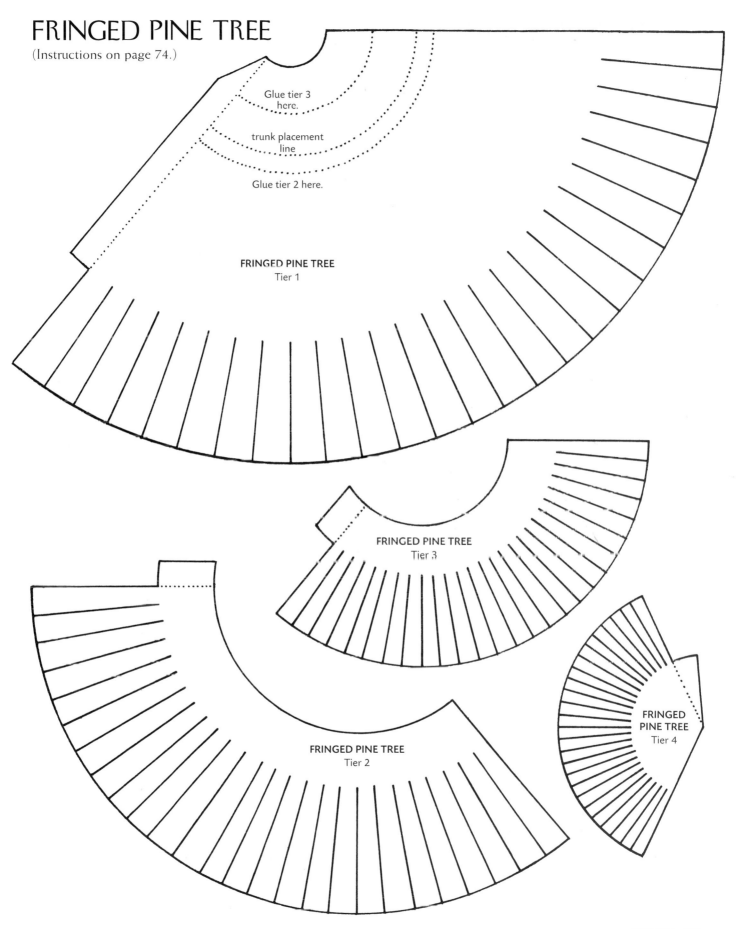

Glue tier 3 here.

trunk placement line

Glue tier 2 here.

FRINGED PINE TREE
Tier 1

FRINGED PINE TREE
Tier 3

FRINGED PINE TREE
Tier 2

FRINGED PINE TREE
Tier 4

COUNTRY CHURCH BOX

(Instructions on pages 72–73.)

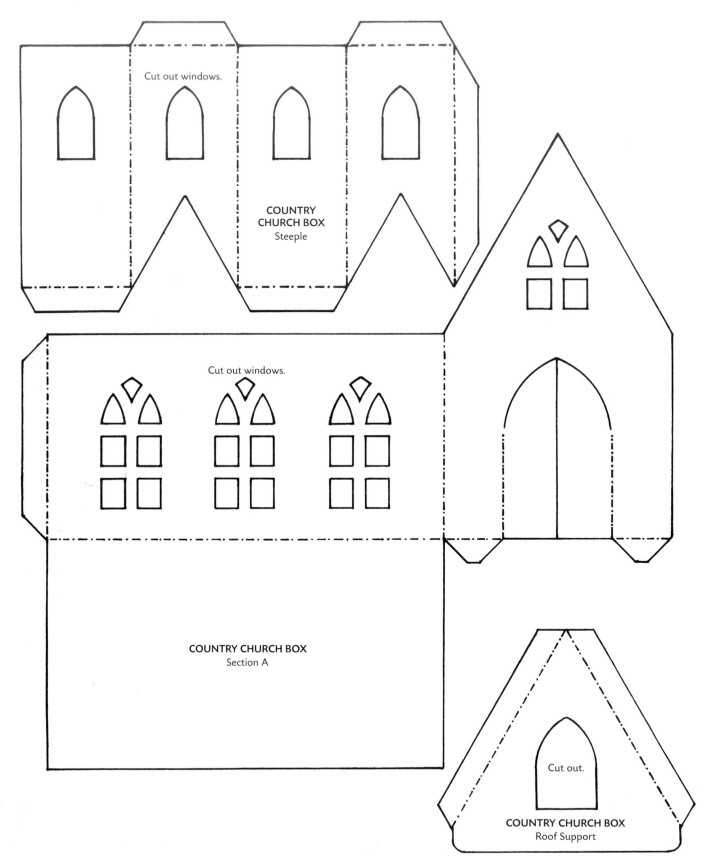

Cut out windows.

COUNTRY CHURCH BOX
Steeple

Cut out windows.

COUNTRY CHURCH BOX
Section A

Cut out.

COUNTRY CHURCH BOX
Roof Support

COUNTRY CHURCH BOX

(continued)

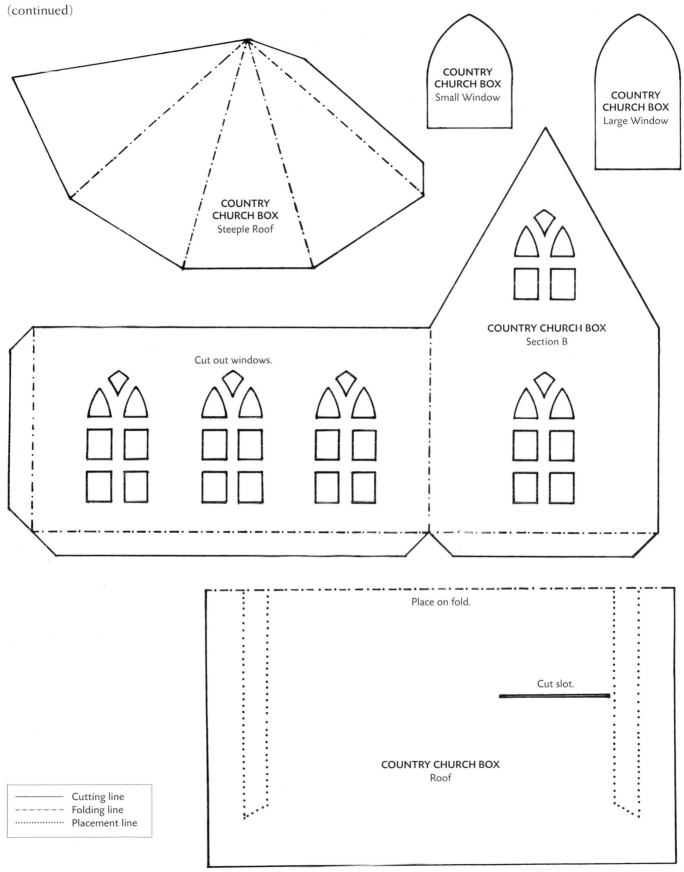

COUNTRY CHURCH BOX
Steeple Roof

COUNTRY CHURCH BOX
Small Window

COUNTRY CHURCH BOX
Large Window

COUNTRY CHURCH BOX
Section B

Cut out windows.

Place on fold.

Cut slot.

COUNTRY CHURCH BOX
Roof

— Cutting line
—·— Folding line
········· Placement line

PETITE PRESENTS

(Instructions on pages 78–79.)

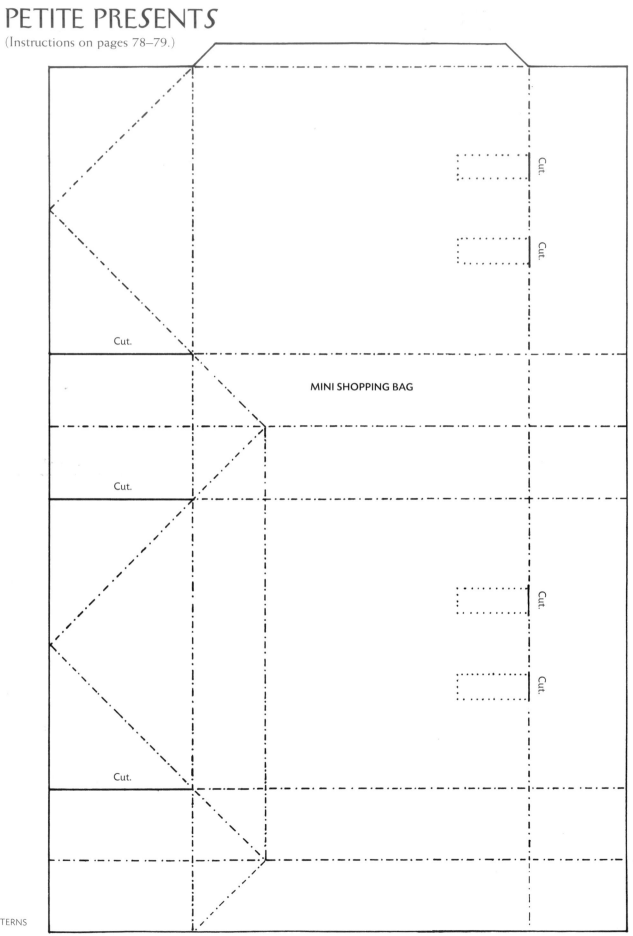

Cut.

Cut.

Cut.

MINI SHOPPING BAG

Cut.

Cut.

Cut.

Cut.

Cut.

PETITE PRESENTS

(continued)

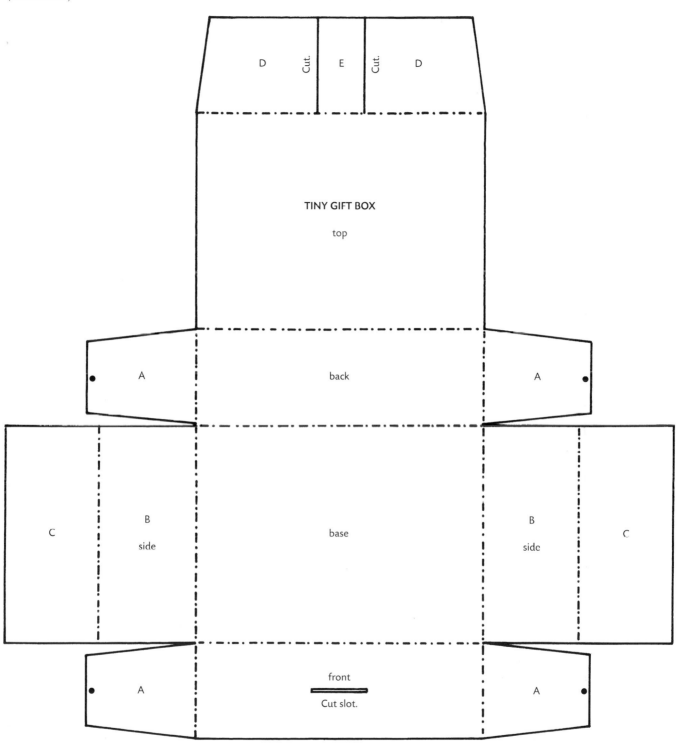

TINY GIFT BOX

top

back

C | B side | base | B side | C

A

A

front

Cut slot.

A

A

D | Cut. | E | Cut. | D

———— Cutting line
—·——·— Folding line
·············· Placement line

CHOIR ANGEL

(Instructions on page 75.)

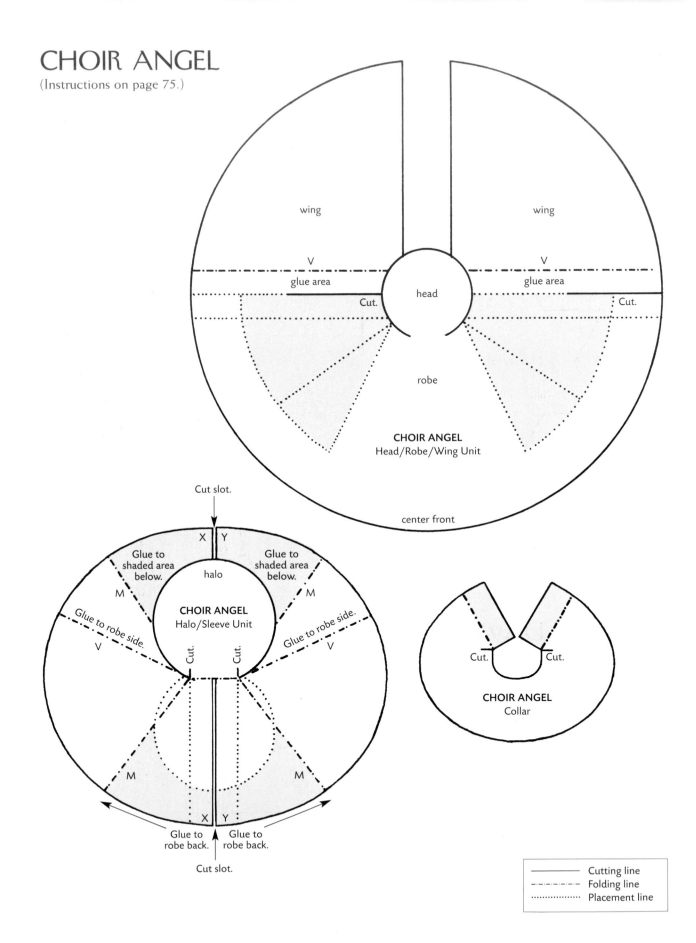

wing

wing

V

V

glue area

glue area

Cut.

head

Cut.

robe

CHOIR ANGEL
Head/Robe/Wing Unit

center front

Cut slot.

X Y

Glue to
shaded area
below.

Glue to
shaded area
below.

halo

M

M

CHOIR ANGEL
Halo/Sleeve Unit

Glue to robe side.

Glue to robe side.

V

V

Cut.

Cut.

M

M

X Y

Glue to
robe back.

Glue to
robe back.

Cut slot.

Cut.

Cut.

CHOIR ANGEL
Collar

———————	Cutting line
—·—·—·—·—	Folding line
·················	Placement line

SPINNING DREIDEL CARD

(Instructions on page 77.)

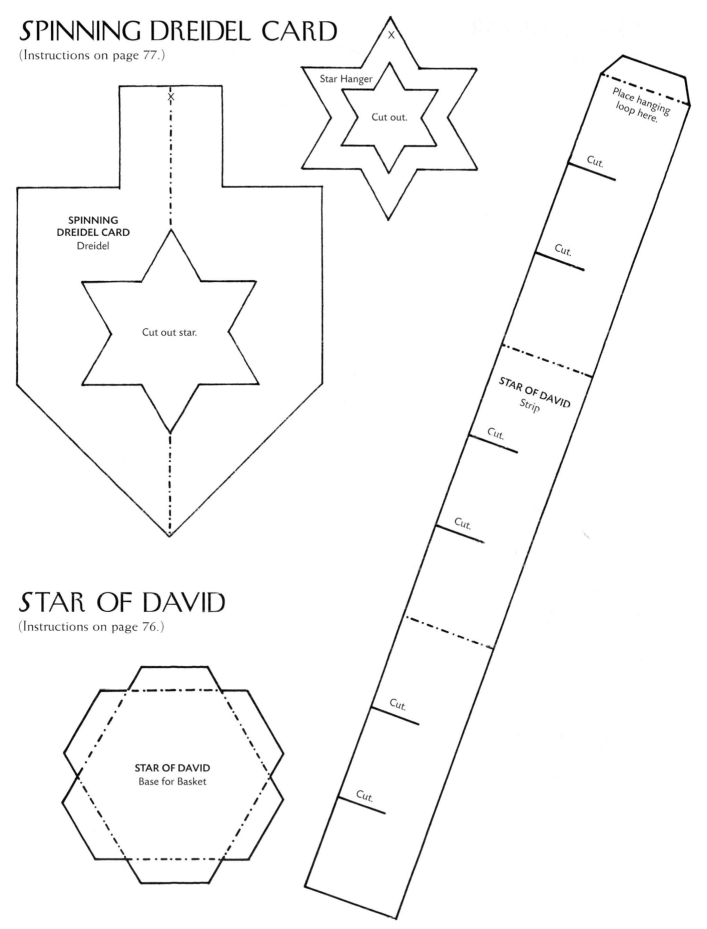

Star Hanger

Cut out.

X

SPINNING DREIDEL CARD
Dreidel

Cut out star.

STAR OF DAVID

(Instructions on page 76.)

STAR OF DAVID
Base for Basket

Place hanging loop here.

Cut.

Cut.

STAR OF DAVID
Strip

Cut.

Cut.

Cut.

Cut.

TRIM-A-TREE CARD
(Instructions on page 83.)

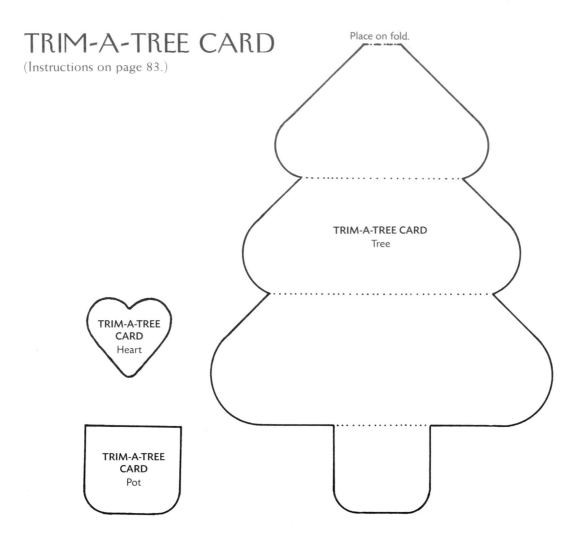

Place on fold.

TRIM-A-TREE CARD
Tree

TRIM-A-TREE CARD
Heart

TRIM-A-TREE CARD
Pot

BOW NAPKIN RING
(Instructions on page 85.)

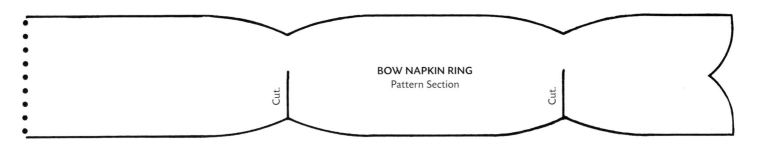

Cut.

BOW NAPKIN RING
Pattern Section

Cut.

———	Cutting line
–·–·–·–	Folding line
··············	Placement line

SANTA CORNUCOPIA

(Instructions on page 82.)

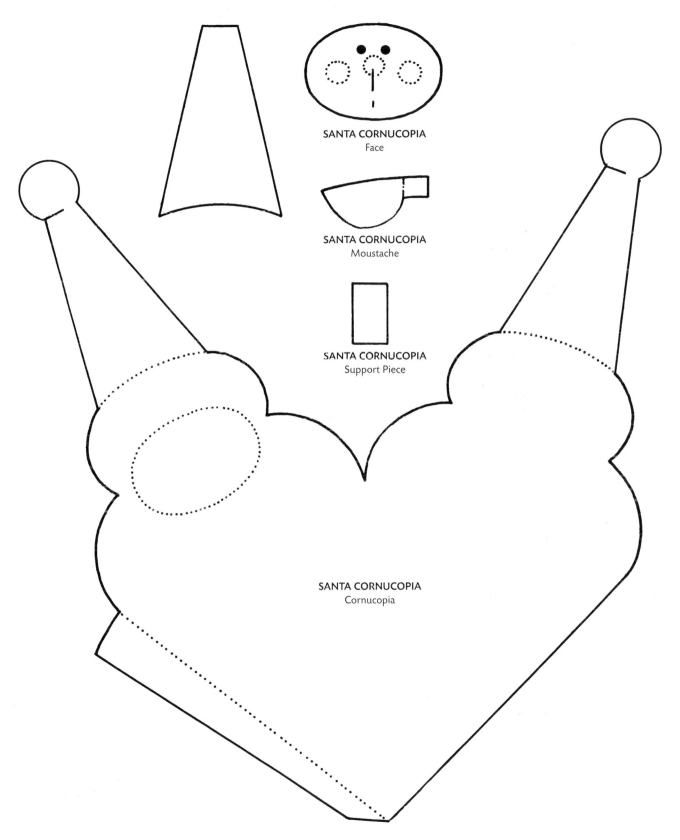

SANTA CORNUCOPIA
Face

SANTA CORNUCOPIA
Moustache

SANTA CORNUCOPIA
Support Piece

SANTA CORNUCOPIA
Cornucopia

PEACE DOVE

(Instructions on page 84.)

MAY 0 5 2004

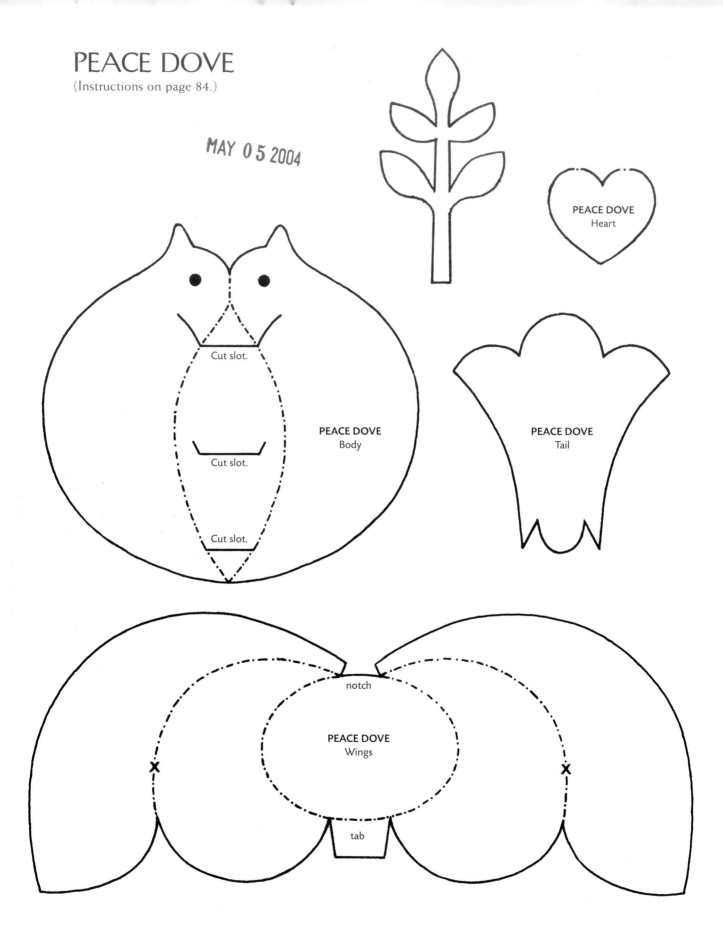

PEACE DOVE
Heart

PEACE DOVE
Body

Cut slot.

Cut slot.

Cut slot.

PEACE DOVE
Tail

notch

PEACE DOVE
Wings

X

X

tab

PASTEL SNOWFLAKES

(Instructions on page 81.)

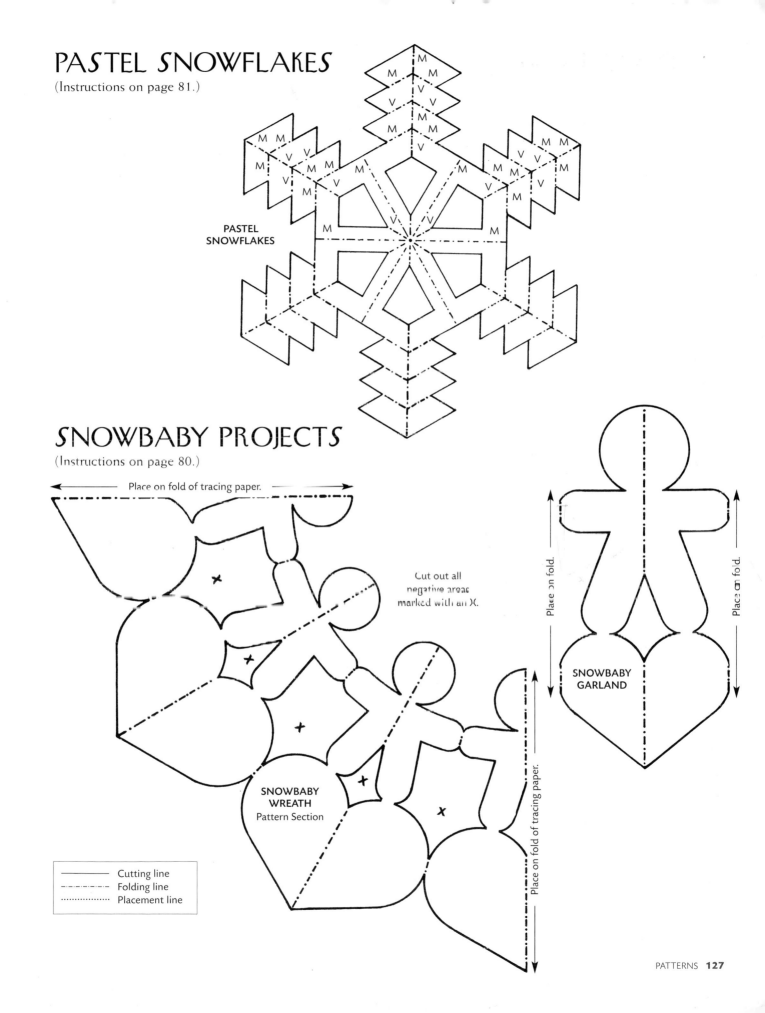

PASTEL
SNOWFLAKES

SNOWBABY PROJECTS

(Instructions on page 80.)

Place on fold of tracing paper.

Cut out all
negative areas
marked with an X.

SNOWBABY
WREATH
Pattern Section

Place on fold of tracing paper.

Place on fold.

Place on fold.

SNOWBABY
GARLAND

———————— Cutting line
—·—·—·—·— Folding line
················· Placement line

INDEX

M304961441   MAY 0 5 2004

The instruction pages for the projects are in bold type. The pattern pages for the projects are in plain type.